Life
Management

Life Management

—Live Better by Working Smarter

Lennart Meynert

OLDCASTLE BUSINESS BOOKS

1989

Oldcastle Books
18 Coleswood Road
Harpenden, Herts AL5 1EQ

Copyright ©1989 by Lennart Meynert

First published by Företagens Utbildningsbyra AB, 1985

British Library Cataloguing in Publishing Record available

ISBN 0 948353 48 1
ISBN 1 874061 11 4 pb

Reprinted 1990
Reprinted 1992

987654

Printed in Great Britain by BPCC Wheatons Ltd, Exeter

The best motivation for improving planning and goal orientation is laziness and a strong need for freedom. A lazy person who loves freedom realizes the value of arranging his or her future in a way that avoids unnecessary work, conflicts, stress and mistakes. Such a person has a better chance of achieving success than a workaholic or career zealot.

— Lennart Meynert

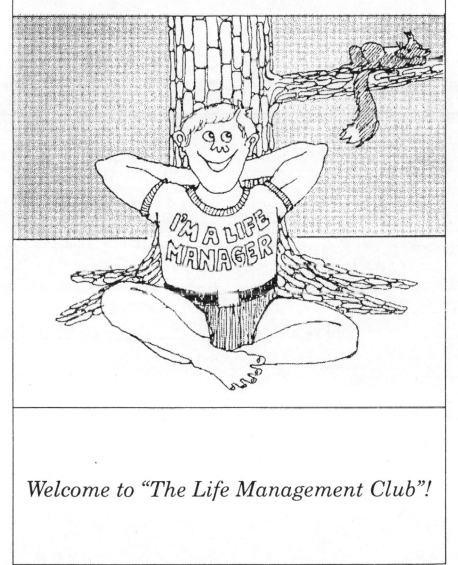

Welcome to "The Life Management Club"!

Part A

Our enormous potential

1   Good news

Welcome

Welcome dear reader to Life Management. Let's start with a little "small talk", so that you get a good idea of what is about to happen.

You can be certain that we are going to have a lot of fun together, and you can also be certain that you won't fall asleep while reading this book. It is stimulating because it is about the most important subject in your life - you. If you would like to learn how to use your abilities to the utmost, this book is filled with good news.

Aha!

While reading this book, you will experience many moments where you will think "Aha!". You will smile to yourself as you recognize the issues and problems discussed within. You will ask yourself why you haven't read about things like this before, and why you haven't discussed these issues with your colleagues.

Put your hand on your watch

Cover the face of your watch, and then try to recall how the number six looks. Think for a moment.

I suppose that you found this task to be harder than you expected, and you probably got it wrong. If this was the case, you are not alone. It is unusual for anyone to get it right, no matter how often you may look at your watch during any hour. The reason is, of course, that you have never had any reason to study the figures in detail. As you will discover while reading this book, a surprising number of our daily routines are carried out in a similar way. With so little conscious thought given to so much of our lives, it is not surprising that we find it difficult or impossible to deal with some parts of our lives.

Increase your awareness

If you think that you are now sure about how the six looks, by the time you complete this book, you will be equally sure about what matters in the future regarding your job and regarding your personal life. This growing awareness will be the basis for our progress together throughout this book.

You will be surprised

One of our most important jobs will be to help open your eyes to clearly see yourself and the realities around you. We shall also encourage you to try different tools and methods designed for life management. Many of these methods will help you use your brain in new and surprisingly powerful ways.

Let me assure you that the author of this book practices what he preaches. Everything that you will discover within these pages has been successfully applied by the author, as well as by many others. These methods can help all sorts of people achieve excellent results. I am not a meticulous person, but in fact rather more on the careless side. I have thought a lot about how people can increase their potential without pushing themselves to a point of discomfort. I think that you will be surprised, as I once were, how easy it is to achieve such goals once you set your mind to them. Surprise will be replaced by enthusiasm when you realize the benefits that you will be able to reap from these techniques.

We are different

The satisfaction that has been the result of our efforts is the driving force behind this book. It is the reason why we want to share our own experiences and the experiences of others with you.

Naturally, we understand that what suits us does not necessarily suit you. We are all different. We must each choose what is best for us from the smorgasbord of ideas set forth in this book. The only thing that we request from you is that you do not reject a technique before trying it out. If you agree to our request, you will achieve rewarding results that otherwise would not have occurred.

What we expect of you

Our goal is that you will come to see yourself as you have never seen yourself before, and discover many new ways to run your life. Imagine what it is like to be able to step off of a treadmill to which you had been chained for years, and to experience new and exciting opportunities in life.

Once you are able to manage your life better, you will be happier, kinder to others, and more confident about yourself. You will have a fuller life, and you won't be so affected by stress. As a result, you will probably be healthier and have a longer life. In addition, this book will give you the techniques to use your unconscious thoughts to help you achieve your goals, by encouraging more spontaneous experiences and greater freedom in your life. Instead of being trapped in situations by stale thoughts, you will be awake, alert, and open to developing and trying new and different ideas. You will begin to use resources around you which had previously been ignored.

You can do something

We will share ideas and tips with you that you can try. Some people may think that the ideas are so simple that it would be embarrassing to write about them. We don't. Experience teaches us that it is the simplest methods which give the best results. Complicated methods that are difficult to follow result only in feelings of guilt and inadequacy. In addition, once you achieve good results with simple methods, you will find it easy to continue with them in the future. The simple rule psychologists call positive reinforcement teaches us that if the results of our actions give us what we want, than it is likely that we will continue to act that way in the future.

Do you have what it takes?

How confidently can you aim for your goals?

This is not an idle question. Not everyone wants to take responsibility for their own life or job. All around you there are people who are controlled more by others than by themselves. They are like rats caught in a cage. They are often unsure of whatever goals they may have, which contributes to even greater uncertainty in their decision-making. They lose interest in many parts of their lives, including their work, and become too tired to regain interests. In time, they become unable to organize what little they have left. In some cases, the only original thoughts these people may have involve thinking up new complaints about their work or their lives.

The situation is not hopeless. In the chapters that follow, you will find the tools to break this destructive pattern, and to successfully progress in your desired direction.

Not a course in career development

This book is not designed to be a course for simply developing careers. It is designed to help you in your life, as well as in your work, and to give you pleasure, as well as information.

Our goal is to help you in your work and in your life to gain more satisfaction and success in what you do, and to gain spare time for other interests as well. You may decide that your family and your spare time are more important than your job. If that is the case, you will achieve even greater skills in arranging your time in the future. You may even decide to develop a career which allows you to stay home, as well. Regardless of your aims, you will be able to reach them more easily.

A leaking boat needs repairing

Whether you want to alter your way of life, or simply to learn something new, it is easier done if it is not connected with tedious and dull work. Yet, books and programs about personal planning often ask participants to map out their present position at work, using complicated plans that must be arranged and analyzed. Most people find this task so boring that they are not motivated to continue. As a result, they may become even more disappointed with themselves, which could be more harmful than if they hadn't taken the program at all.

This book is based on a different way of thinking: It makes no sense to record on a piece of paper the amount of water that is pouring into a leaking boat. The only thing that makes sense is to repair the obvious damage and get the boat seaworthy again. In the same way, if you are dissatisfied with your present job, or if you often feel exhausted as a result of misusing your energy, this book will provide you with the tools you need to repair the damage. As often as not, the resources that you need to repair the damage are already within your grasp, although you may probably be unaware that they are there.

Flight of the bumblebees

You can learn how to control your life so that you can achieve more, and at the same time, increase your free time. You can learn how to get these results in the same way you learn how to drive a car or to play golf. Don't think, however, that it is easy.

When you first learn how to drive or to play golf, you become aware of the problems that must be overcome. But awareness alone is not enough. Your ability to work creatively to achieve your goal will determine how well you will succeed in your projects. With the proper knowledge and training, learning new skills is fun, effective, and gratifying. Without the proper knowledge and training, your chances of succeeding in controlling the many complications that can effect your life is about as likely as waking up one morning and being able to play "Flight Of The Bumblebees" on your newly bought violin.

Caught by the police

Nobody but you is responsible for how you use your time. It's easy to try to blame your boss, peers, subordinates or organization in order to excuse your own failings. It is understandable to try this, but it is a lie. It is also easy to try to hide behind simple blanket statements like "I just can't do it", "I'm not good enough", "I have a poor memory", or "I have no self control". Inventing excuses is easy, but getting yourself and others to believe them may often become a difficult job. Once the excuses are stripped away, what remains is that you are responsible for the choices you make.

When you drive a car, you are responsible for controlling it. If you go through a red light, excuses will not prevent a ticket. The police will not accept an explanation that you had a lapse in memory because of an argument you had with a friend. If we are to manage our lives better, we must first accept the facts when we fail in our responsibilities, and realize the consequences of our own actions.

What are the consequences when we make a mistake in deciding which job to take on at work? Will we get caught by the police? Hardly! Punishment is unlikely. As the margins of error are pretty wide in most jobs, we can probably continue on as we did before. However, the odds of being offered more stimulating and exciting work will be slimmer, as will be the chance for promotions.

A carpenter without a hammer

As we noted before, you can learn how to use time and resources so that it is easier to work in a more relaxed way, and still manage to achieve better results in a shorter time. The easiest way to learn is to be motivated towards a goal. The fact that you have this book in front of you demonstrates how interested you are in finding the necessary tools to reach your goals. Only by using the right tools can we work in a better way.

Even if it were possible to change your personality, there is no need to do so. Too many books waste your time by demanding that you must change your personality in one way or another. This book is not one of them. You will always be the same person that you basically are right now. The only person you will spend your entire life with is yourself. There is no choice but to learn to live with your unique personality.

You should not be depressed by this fact. Instead, be glad that you are a unique person with lots of marvelous qualities, as well as some less marvelous ones. You are what you are. If you get to know yourself better, and learn how to use the right tools to help you achieve your goal, then happiness, reduced stress, and a more creative life will follow. Without the right tools for meeting

A carpenter without a hammer. What tools do you use?

your needs, you are like a carpenter without a hammer. Few people would accept the work of a carpenter who uses a butter-knife as a screwdriver and a rock as a hammer. Yet so many people expect to handle difficult situations that come up in life simply by waking up every morning, and wishing that everything will work out fine.

Ripples in water

How effective are the tools that you use to manage your work and your life?

One test is to ask yourself how you feel when you are working. Do you really have the right tools to achieve the results you want? We find it easy to accept that the carpenter, the hairdresser, the gardener and the farmer must have special equipment to assist them in their jobs. But if you are a lawyer, a teacher, a corporate manager or a merchant, you may assume that you can work out whatever problems some up without depending upon any special tools. Indeed, in some situations you may be able to. But sooner or later you come to realize that there must be better ways to accomplish what is important to you. If this is the case, this book is written for you.

Within these pages you will discover tools that are suitable for your needs. Included are practical applications of techniques that can energize you, open your mind to new points of view, and modify attitudes that may have been working against you. Once you begin applying these tools to reach your goals, you will find yourself becoming increasingly positive, and under reduced stress. Every step you take forward will have a positive influence on other seemingly unrelated aspects of your life. These good effects will spread like ripples in water, both within you and around you. You will still be the same person, but both you and your environment will be more in harmony.

Break your own chains first

We must first be concerned with how well you direct your own work. You may be a manager who is responsible for a number of employees. If you are to succeed as a manager for others, it is first necessary to be able to direct yourself and your own work. A manager who cannot handle his or her own problems can never become a great manager.

Your most troublesome co-worker

Among all of your co-workers, there is one who is especially troublesome. Nobody is as obstinate and as stubborn as this co-worker. However much you nag and threaten this person, sometimes nothing seems to help. You may often find yourself losing your patience with this co-worker. Certain things just don't get done. This co-worker, of course, is you.

Even if you do not manage other employees, you are still your own boss. You are responsible to and for yourself, which is not as easy as it sounds. It is certain, for example, that you have chores at home which need doing, and which you ought to have done years ago, but which are still left unfinished. We will use a number of tools to help you accomplish what you want to get done. These tools are designed to help you gain a greater control over your own life. They will help you to reduce the conflicts you may have between you and your most troublesome co-worker.

What is Life Management?

Life Management is a system designed to give you control over your life. It is a complete approach for managing your work and your personal life.

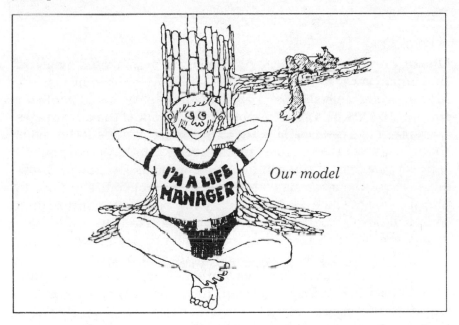

Our model

It is different from Time Management, a term that often tends to confuse more than it clarifies. The notion that time can be directed is an illusion. Time is constant and cannot be influenced. It is, however, possible to direct your own life. This is our starting point.

We are not out to change your personality. It is almost as impossible to influence as time. But we will modify your patterns of behaviour. Together, we will achieve great things, with surprisingly little effort once we learn how to use the proper tools.

The author of this book have spent decades in the practice and theory of developing organizations and managers. Over and over, I have determined that every organization is able to improve its profitability if workers learn how to direct their work in better ways. There is no need for special equipment, or changes in the organizational structure to achieve these results. If the members of the organization can learn to choose the right tasks, resources will be made available, and creative activities will increase. This will have a positive effect on the energy level within the entire organization, which in turn can generate new and exciting goals.

Freud's gift
One of Freud's greatest contributions was to make us aware of the importance of the unconscious in governing our actions. Many psychologists believe that about eighty percent of our thinking occurs on a subconscious level. Think of the advantages we might have if we could learn to make use of our subconscious thoughts. Over the decades, psychotherapists have determined that we give a lot of thought on a subconscious level to our problems. These thoughts may often include appropriate solutions to our problems, which we may or may not be able to capture on a conscious level. Imagine what it would be like if we could harness this activity of our brain. If we could utilize this worthwhile source, our creative abilities would increase dramatically.

One of the gains you achieve while developing your life management skills is to bring your subconscious thoughts to the service of your conscious mind.

Down to earth

We will not be very theoretical. Determining the goals of life is not the subject of this book. Stacks of books have already been written about such aims. On the contrary, we shall be very down to earth, focusing on the tools that we need, and how they can be used to help us achieve our goals. As a result of working better, we can increase our awareness of ourselves and our surrounding world. This increased self-knowledge may help us catch up with other interests both in our work and in our private life. Only then we will have time to speculate over life's important questions, which may influence new goals we may choose to follow.

Choosing the right job

As leaders and developers of management programs, we sometimes find it hard to make a message clear, especially when we talk about the need to plan. Every group has at least one participant who assumes that people who use planning skills must lead boring and tied-up lives, with few opportunities for freedom and natural experiences.

We have experienced many difficulties arguing against the point of view, even though we clearly knew we were right. Only by planning one's future could one avoid repetitious discomfort, misunderstandings, fire fighting and unwanted surprises. But we could not succeed in convincing the opponents of planning. Nowadays we are more successful. We have come to understand that we and our opponents had not been talking the same language with reference to the meaning of the term planning. By planning, our opponents meant starting with a given amount of time available for work, dividing that time into smaller units, and then filling those units up with work until they were fully occupied. Of course, they felt the same about planning as they would about being fitted for a straight-jacket.

To us, planning means something totally different. Planning means choosing what you want to do. When we plan, we choose the jobs necessary to achieve the results we want. We could choose to stop working on a project that is no longer of importance to us. On the other hand, when we have decided that something is important, we could choose to schedule it into our day.

The difference between these two outlooks is enormous. Our starting point is a task, while our opponents' starting point is time itself. Once this is understood disputes can be worked out. Without task planning, the result is chaos. As our opponents and we have discovered, chaos and freedom are not the same thing.

If time were not so short

As we have said, it is an illusion to think that time can be controlled. Time is a resource. Within its limits, it is possible to choose the right jobs to do. Those who complain that they are short of time often live with the illusion that their problems could be solved if they were given more time. They are wrong! If they were given more time, they would still be unable to solve their problems. They would continue to work in the same ineffective way they had before, failing to choose to do those activities that are most important to them.

Even if a person actually does have too many important things to do, there are still benefits in learning how to consciously choose what to take on first. As you learn what is really important, you can decide to restructure your work and your life, developing your own world in ways that are best for you.

The good old prehistoric days are gone

Let's take a close look at an interesting phenomenon.

We all know people who refuse to write notes to remind themselves about anything, regardless of the consequences. They would rather make several extra trips to the market, or think up ways of defending themselves for forgetting to buy various items, than to write a shopping list. Intuitively, we forgive these people with the phrase "They are only human".

It is quite possible that planning is an activity that people do not take to naturally. The further back we go in history, the more we discover that humans tend to be more activity-oriented than thought-oriented. Prehistoric man had less of a need for planning than modern man. In prehistoric times, life centered around the present, with its immediate danger and pleasures.

Today, life has become more complicated. The desire to take immediate actions must often give way to planning for more distant events. As it is true that we no longer live in prehistoric times, it is also true that planning does not come to us naturally. In the age we live in, to get what we want we must first learn how to plan.

A boxer's footwork

It is interesting how a term used by boxers, "footwork", can often be substituted for the word "planning". Boxers develop their footwork to put themselves in the best positions for taking actions, for dealing with unexpected blows, and for gaining control in anticipation of upcoming opportunities. Good footwork sets up conditions where they are motivated to strike out with all they have got.

With good footwork, you are less likely to blindly reach for goals that have been put up in front of you. You are more likely to be flexible, curious, and creative regarding the world around you. You will be better able to go after the opportunities that will help you develop throughout your entire life. With the right footwork, you remain more in control of situations. You stay keenly aware of both problems and opportunities that surround you.

Yet planning is more than just footwork. The tasks we choose to take on as a result of our planning may lead to new and exciting situations that we had never before imagined, both for ourselves and for the organizations we work for.

Motherhood, planning, and apple pie

The notion that a manager must set goals, and develop plans to meet those goals is in the same category as motherhood and apple pie. It sounds too good to be questioned. Still, it must be said that this notion is too simplistic. We know that in reality managers generally do not plan their day to day work. They tend to do what they have to do depending on what is expected of them at the time. They try to achieve the best results possible within their own areas of responsibility. At times, of course, they

21

must reconsider what they are doing. At such times, it may be necessary for them to redefine their aims.

Management studies demonstrates that important planning is often neglected. In one study of 500 American managers, 72 percent claimed that they had no time to plan, in terms of choosing their tasks. As they had no time to plan for the future, they were less prepared to deal with unforeseen circumstances, including delays, errors, misunderstandings, conflicts, and fluctuations in costs.

If planning for the future is as important as most managers believe, and if it should be included in the daily routine of every office worker, why is it so rarely done? One reason that we mentioned earlier was that many people have a misconceived notion about what planning really is. Another reason may be that planning is thought by many people as being an overwhelmingly serious event that they may not have the right skills for. As long as we carry around the idea that we do not have the right skills for planning, or that we can only plan when conditions are just right for such important work, no planning will occur.

Chaos!

Let us not make mountains out of molehills. Planning is simply a tool to help us with our daily routines, and to help us deal with the future. It should be a routine activity, rather than a special event.

If it were not for this tool, life would be chaotic. A chaotic environment has no room for creative thoughts or work. It only encourages messy situations or tough restrictions. Planning, on the other hand, encourages freedom.

By planning, we increase the chances that our lives will run smoothly. When this happens, our ability to tackle everyday problems increases, and we have more freedom to do other things. Planning may not come naturally to people, but the alternatives to planning, chaos and slavery, are unacceptable.

Your work and your home life, together again

As you may have noticed, it is becoming more and more difficult to separate your work from your private life.

It is fair to say that the responsibilities you have in your personal life are no less important than those you have in you work life. A working spouse is expected to have his or her work organized well enough so that the share of the work he or she is responsible for will be done after coming home.

As you become more successful, you collect more things. The more you have, the more you are responsible for. More and more work is needed to cope with the new things you collect, whether they are cars, boats, vacation homes, or collections of electronic equipment. Yet, the responsibilities you may have in your personal life are often not looked upon as being as important as those in your professional life. Some people attempt to cope with this misconception by going to the opposite extreme of always putting their personal or family life before their work life.

As a result of too little attention and planning given so one part of your life or another, breakdowns can occur. When breakdowns do occur, they can lead to a number of unforeseen problems, including deteriorating relationships, unnecessary extra expenses, stress, misunderstandings and moodiness. It should be possible to have a good private or family life, and to have a satisfying work life as well. This goal can be achieved through effective planning. In this book, we will spend a good deal of time getting your home life sorted out, as well as your work life. You can look forward to an exciting new experience.

The danger of stress

We all need some level of stress to keep life interesting. But when the stress in our lives reaches a level that is not right for us, the resulting distress can lead to problems that may include illness. More and more studies demonstrate how destructive levels of stress can lower our immunity system levels, increasing the likelihood of disease. By gaining control over our lives we can expect to experience less stress, which will contribute to better health. This book will provide you with a number of excellent techniques for reducing unnecessary stress.

Laziness - a desirable quality

Have you ever met a person who is lazy but responsible, and also has a strong will to be free? That person probably uses energy in an economical and goal oriented way. Such a person aims for successful results. One of his or her best qualities is courage. It takes courage to aim for successful results. For most people, it is much easier to just work, regardless of the amount of work they may have to do or what they can gain from it.

Imagine that a manager is sitting in his office thinking. This particular day he has had some good ideas which have given him some satisfaction, but he has not yet reached any conclusions. His colleague is sitting in the room next door. He is working frantically on a report. The report contains some satisfactory conclusions. The problem is that no one will ever read the report, or show even the remotest interest in it.

Which of these colleagues is the most valuable? Is it the one who spends time thinking or the one who toils in the sweat of his brow? Most of us would sympathize with the toiler. But is that fair? Is it not more difficult to quest after thoughtful ideas that may benefit the organization than to routinely carry out activities that lead nowhere?

You can't please everyone

Not everyone can benefit from this book. There are people who will neither be willing to simplify or improve their work, nor make it more goal oriented. They are satisfied with their own picture of themselves. Perhaps they believe that looking busy brings a sense of status. Perhaps they believe that to be thought of as important or irreplaceable they must look busy. Even if these people could change their way of working, the spare time they would get might make them uncomfortable. For these people, catching up on their work might mean that they would have to start work on a new and perhaps difficult or boring job.

Why anyone would want to work in a way which is filled with stress, errors, fire fighting, complaints, unnecessary steps, and the like is beyond our understanding. Such conditions give little room for spontaneity or good working relationships. Quite clearly, life is much easier once you can gain control of your own work.

What is wrong with the obvious?

This book contains much which you might think is obvious. But to tell you the obvious is not the aim of this book. Instead, the aim of this book is much more difficult. It is to get you to **do** what is obvious.

Cut working hours for better management

One of the greatest obstacles to managing in an efficient way is the excessive amount of time available for us to do our work. The average person works eight hours a day, five days a week. This offers enormous possibilities when it comes to time. People who work under stress often think that they are short of time. In reality, their main problem may actually be the excessive amount of time available for work.

Such problems can be solved in a variety of ways. They could work in a more relaxed way and with greater concentration on results if they were forced to shorten their work week by a day or two. By doing so, they are forced to take a close look at their situation at work. New and more efficient methods and routines would have to be devised. Work would have to be delegated. As a result of having to actively plan their work, they would be able to accomplish more during the shorter time that they have available. In addition, they now have two free days a week. This time could be used for golf, tennis, household activities, or taking care of the children.

Like you, we know people who are always short of time. In the case of one person a major factor was that he had never had a reason to question what he was doing. One day he was forced to do so. An associate had become ill, putting him in the position of having to do the work of two people. He locked himself in his room for a weekend to think and plan. It worked! In spite of having to manage the work of two people, he was able to work under less stress, and to have more spare time as well.

Enough "small talk"

Now that we have finished with our introduction, we would like to wish you the best of luck in your efforts to improve your everyday way of life. If you are successful, the next few months will seem as enjoyable as a summer vacation. You will be free at last to enjoy the exciting experiences you have chosen for yourself. Life will work out as you want it to after all!

Every day should be enjoyed as if you were on a summer vacation

2   The ultimate resource - your incredible brain

The future

Some time ago, ten winners of the Nobel prize were asked the following question: "In what scientific area do you think the greatest advances will be made in the years ahead?" The majority of them answered "brain research". Much of what we know today about how our brain works comes from Sperry, the great American researcher who was awarded the Nobel prize in medicine in early 1980's.

Two roots

Many techniques discussed in this book have been inspired by developments from research on the human brain. Techniques have also been inspired by developments in other areas, particularly stress reduction. As you will discover, these areas of study have several things in common. For one, the more relaxed you are when working, the easier it will be to use the capacity of your brain more fully.

That ain't peanuts

You have a fantastic brain. Throughout your life, you have the opportunity to challenge its limits, develop its abilities, and put it to good use. You can take advantage of these opportunities by learning how to use some very simple tools.

It has been estimated that there are approximately ten billion neurons in the brain. Every neuron has thousands of synapses, from which impulses are transmitted from neuron to neuron. That means that the possible number of connections that may exist between nerve cells is 10 followed by 800 zeros. We can give you an idea of the size of the number of connections we are dealing with, when you consider that the total number of atoms in the known universe has been estimated to be 10 followed by 100 zeros. The number that represents all of the atoms in the known universe is just peanuts compared to the dimensions in which your brain could be described. The net telephone system of the entire world can hardly be compared to the complexity of your brain.

For each of us, the most enormous resource we can ever use is within our own head. Until now, you may have used no more than a fraction of your brain's capacity. But with the techniques you are about to discover, you can learn to use your resources more than ever before.

The two hemispheres

As you probably already know, the human brain has two hemispheres or sides, the right hemisphere and the left hemisphere. Each side has different functions. The ancient Egyptians knew that the left side of the brain controls the right side of the body, and that the right side of the brain controls the left side of the body.

More recently, scientists have discovered that each of the hemispheres of the brain also control a number of other functions. These functions include specific types of thinking skills, including mathematical skills, speaking skills, creative functions, linguistic skills, and logic. By studying the effects of different diseases, Sperry found that different sides of the brain were active, depending on the activity that a subject was involved in. The left side of the brain becomes active, for example, when we are involved in solving a mathematical problem. The right side of the brain becomes active when we are asked to identify various colors. Logical and mathematical calculations are worked out in the left side of the brain. Problems requiring artistic or creative thought are solved by the right hemisphere of the brain.

Sperry also determined that each side of the brain has its own conscious thoughts and memories. Each side works according to its own principles. The left side is logical and functions in thought sequences; the right side functions by using parallel thinking associations. Another particularly significant difference is that the left side of the brain is verbal; it thinks through words. The right hemisphere, on the other hand, thinks through pictures.

The functions of each side of the brain

Listed below are some of the functions controlled by each side of the human brain. The results reported in the list are found to be true for most people, except in the case of 30 percent of left-handed individuals, where the center of speech is found to be located in the right hemisphere of the brain rather than in the left hemisphere.

Left side

Logical thinking
Speech
Mathematical calculations
Analysis of details
Relations of time
Critical evaluations

Right side

Imagination
Creativity
Cubic thinking
Rhythm

Music
Recognition of colors
Emotions
Visual patterns perception
Holistic thinking
Dealing with similarities and relationships

Mostly the left side

Twentieth century Western culture tends to encourage thinking which takes place in the left side of the brain, and discourage thinking which takes place in the right side of the brain. Our schools and work environments tend to reward and encourage individuals who show talent in physics and mathematics, rather than those who show talent in "elective courses" such as art or music. Imagination and creativity are often supported with lip service in our culture, but are rarely rewarded in our daily lives. As a result of the limited support given to its nonverbal functions, the right side of the brain is often neglected in our society. As the ability to solve problems, think creatively, experience empathy, and express feeling can be discouraged easily, this is a serious problem.

If we could learn how to make better use of the right side of our brain, we would be able to open ourselves up to new opportunities, leading ourselves further away from the monotonous every day situations people so often find themselves trapped in. We could counteract the tendency to be dominated by a single side of the brain. As we learn to use the right side of our brain, we can increase our creativity and problems solving ability.

Some researchers have raised the intriguing possibility that in prehistoric times, there was a much greater need to use the right side of the brain than there is today. Prehistoric man had to be able to determine direction without a map, to sense danger, and to interpret changes in the environment. As civilization became more and more complex, the need for logical and analytic abilities became increasingly important. This may have contributed to modern man's dependency on the left side of the brain. Our modern society has continued to grow more complex. Logic and analytic abilities can no longer be the only faculties we must depend upon. It may be that we must again learn to rely more on intuitive abilities for survival.

Cubic thought

We have listed cubic thought as a function of the right side of the brain. Two examples can be given to demonstrate the vital importance of this function.

Imagine two boys throwing a ball in a gale. The wind is blowing hard, yet they seem to have no serious problem throwing or catching the ball. Their ability to adapt to the changing conditions in the environment, and to adjust their muscle actions to changing conditions occurs automatically. It is not through analytical, logical calculations of the left side of the brain. that such elegant, accurate, and rapid adjustments are done, but rather through cubic, holistic, intuitive decisions made by the right side of the brain.

Studies of individuals whose right hemisphere has been damaged reveal what life would be like without the cubic and holistic functions of the brain. These individuals become unable to identify where they are located. They cannot find their way home. Even when at home, they feel unsure about where they are. As important as cubic thought is for our survival, its existence remains unrecognized by most people.

Improving your golf

You can develop the abilities of the right side of your brain, as well as the left side. You have already done so if you have ever tried to develop your athletic abilities. Few people attempt to improve their golf game, for example, by spending time intellectually analyzing their mistakes. Instead, they watch professional golf players in action, to gain a "sense" of how they play. When we actually swing the golf club, success comes when the critical, analyzing left side of the brain gives way to the imaginative, holistic right side of the brain to guide the shot.

Improving your tennis

What is true for improving a game of golf is also true for improving a game of tennis. Experts know that films showing brilliant tennis players can be very useful for improving an average player's form. Good players know that when they go to swing at the ball, they do better when they can shut off their critical analyzing functions that could get in the way of a natural, relaxed swing. Boring instructions about how to hold a racket, how to stand, or how to move one's body may have caused more people to quit the game than any other reason. Excessive criticism about inaccurate shots do not produce better tennis players either.

Pros have discovered that to improve tennis skills you must first subdue the functions of the left side of the brain. Your game will not improve if you become anxious about hitting the ball when it comes to your side of the court. To keep yourself from becoming anxious you can say the word "bounce" out loud as the ball lands on your side of the court, and "hit" as your racket comes into contact with the ball. As it is not possible to consciously experience more than one thought at a time, by concentrating on the words "bounce" and "hit", you can stop your mind from wandering to thoughts that might interfere with your game. If you are a tennis player, you might find this technique worth a try. If you are not a tennis player, you can gain an understanding of how performance can be improved by reducing an overbearing function on the left hemisphere of the brain.

A superior memory for images

The right side of the brain is nonverbal; it functions and remembers in images. This nonverbal memory has a number of advantages over verbal memory. If you were asked what you did last summer, a number of images might emerge in your mind. At that point, you might consciously put the images into some order, and select a group of images you wish to recall.

The ability to make better use of the right and left hemispheres of your brain can be learned. Yet few schools or management courses attempt to show you how the images many of your thoughts and memories are made of can be used to your advantage at work, or in your personal life. This is true in spite of the fact that memory experts have spoken about the advantages of visual memory for decades. It has long been known, for example, that it is easier to memorize a list of names, numbers, or written material by first "translating" the verbal contents into a series of images, and letting your imagination flow to connect the images into an unforgettable sequence of events.

In chapter three we will discuss a technique for capturing the creative functions on the right side of your brain in ways that can be routinely used by the left side of the brain.

An exciting experiment

In order to gain a better understanding about the two sides of the brain, Sperry studied patients whose brain stems had been severed. The brain stem, which is composed of billions of nerve fibers, connects the two hemisphere s of the brain. By preventing communication between the hemispheres of seriously damaged epileptics, the epileptic symptoms of the patients seemed to be considerably reduced.

Curiously, if a person whose brain stem has been severed is blindfolded and given an object in his right hand, he will have no difficulty in identifying that object. As you will recall, the center of speech is located on the left side of the brain. If that same person is then given an object in his left hand, he will be unable to identify it. His left hand is steered by the nonverbal right side of his brain. Once communication with the left side of the brain containing the center of speech is broken, the patient cannot identify the object. However, the patient can still select the object he has held in his left hand from a collection of objects.

Recognizing people

When you stop to think about it, recognizing a person you may have seen only once before is rather fantastic. It is a tribute to the enormous capacities of the right side of your brain that you can take this ability in your stride. A vast amount of information has to be absorbed and stored so that you might recognize a person once again.

Would you buy a used car from this man?

Imagine returning to your home after test driving a second hand car that you decided not to buy. You may have been satisfied with the car, but some impression you had about the dealer stopped you from buying it. You may find it impossible to put into words what disturbed you about the dealer. When pressed, you might rationalize that perhaps it was the way he looked, perhaps it was the way he behaved, or perhaps it was just a general impression that you had. Whatever it was, you came to an intuitive decision that you did not want to buy the car from him.

Your eye-movements reveal you

Physiologists have noted that they can determine which side of the brain is active by observing various eye-movements and directions of focus. For example, you generally look to the right when the left side of your brain is active. On the other hand, you will look to the left when solving a cubic problem, as when giving a person directions to a destination. While listening to someone during a conversation, you often look directly at that person. When answering that person, you often look away to the right, as the center of speech in the left hemisphere is at work.

You may find it interesting to catch your own eye movements in various situations.

A difference between men and women

The result of research comparing men and women suffering from the same types of brain damage support the hypothesis that there is a difference between the functions of the brain for men and for women. It is hypothesized that both sides of the brain of the female work in more similar ways than the sides of the brain of the male, which tend to be more specialized.

There is also evidence that communication between the hemisphere of the female is better developed. Some researchers have speculated that women tend to use their brain in a more balanced way while men are more inclined to use either their right or their left side of the brain. Perhaps men are more likely to adopt a singular outlook, while women more easily adapt a holistic view. This better coordination and balance of the female brain could be an explanation of what is commonly called "female intuition".

Although it is true that historically women have not had the same opportunities to use their resources as have men, the proportion of "specialists" who are female in almost every field seems surprisingly small. The role of the parts of the brain in influencing a choice of careers in specialist versus generalist areas could use further examination.

The sides of the brain working together

The left side of the brain contains the center of speech. It works in a logical, cool and clear manner. The right side works according to principles of intuition. We may conclude that a man like Albert Einstein had a well developed left hemisphere, while Beethoven had a well developed right hemisphere. But it should be added that Einstein was an able violin player, and Beethoven was a capable logical thinker. This supports our premise that it is important to achieve a sound balance between the two sides of the brain.

Developing musical, artistic and physical skills have a positive influence on other abilities as well, including problem solving abilities. Educators have demonstrated that children who have difficulties in reading and writing will improve when they receive training in physical activities. Rudolph Steiner's educational ideas, for example, which are the roots of the Waldorf schools have been praised for their effectiveness for over 60 years. In such programs, education leans heavily towards rhythmics, music, singing, and imaginative story telling. The child's hands are trained along with the brain. The time children spend playing, acting, in sports and in artistic activities, is considered to be well spent, contributing equally to the total development of the individual.

Whatever age you may be, it is to your advantage to reduce the dependency you may have on the left side of your brain by giving the right side of your brain greater opportunities to be involved in your conscious decision making.

Stuttering

We need not go into much more detail about how the hemispheres of our brain function. More detailed information is becoming available in literature. Our aim is to provide an awareness that the two sides of the brain work in different ways, and that our thought processes work in different ways as well. Thinking can be logical and calculated, as well as relaxed and creative.

A participant in one of our programs shared with us the fact that he had a child who stuttered. As is typical, the child had no stuttering problems when singing. He was an excellent singer. The causes for stuttering are still not known. But it is interesting to note that singing, rhythm, and musical appreciation are most often dominated by the right side of the brain, while speech is dominated by the left side of the brain. Perhaps, when a stutterer sings, competition between the two sides of the brain is reduced.

Different professions - different functions of the brain

Certain professions may attract individuals who are dominated by one or the other side of the brain. Artists, painters, musicians and athletes are most probably dominated by the right side of their brains. They have a "feeling" for what they are doing. A singer or musician may be said to have "soul". An artist becomes detached during the act of creation. It is often impossible to reach a writer who is writing.

People dominated by the right side of the brain are often characterized as engrossed in profound concentration. Artists are often stereotyped as being uncommunicative. Many athletes have the same reputation. It is an event when the press finds an athlete who interviews well. On the other hand, there are craftsmen who spend most of their time talking and theorizing. Through their language they create a reality we may find hard to understand. We have all come into contact with bureaucrats and politicians who lack the ability to judge the realism of their ideas and decisions. This to may be explained by a dependency on certain brain functions at the expense of other functions.

For better or for worse, most of us are dominated by the left side of our brain. Fortunately, it is probably easier to improve skills associated with the right hemisphere, than the other way around.

Children's drawings

Parents and teachers are often astonished by the development of their children's drawings. When they first learn how to draw, children demonstrate a level of creativity and originality which is often attributed to great works of art.

Generally, the right side of the brain dominates the activities of young children. After a few years at school, their natural artistic skills are often significant reduced. In our culture, schools place increasing importance on logic, realism, and detail. The efforts of the left side of the brain receive greater reinforcement than the right side. As the child's language skills continue to develop, the left hemisphere often begins to dominate activities. To some extent, this may be due to the pressures put on children by our society and our schools.

Moments of trance

At times, we may become more or less detached from the world around us. We have discussed how artists and writers often gravitate to this state when they are creating. Even if you are not an artist, now and then you may feel a need for this detachment. As you will see, it is possible to reach this helpful condition on your own. This condition, in which your mind is dominated by the right side of your brain, can occur when you are engaged in activities that are routine and monotonous, as well as when you are totally involved in some project.

People who excel in various types of sports strive to achieve this state. The monotonous thudding of jogger's feet, and the equally monotonous view of passing trees, allow many athletes to experience visual bubbles of thought, which now and again reach their consciousness. As such moments, an individual may be extremely creative. Perhaps you may recall such an experience, in which you were able to solve a difficult problem, or see

37

entirely new alternatives to the way you carry out your everyday activities.

You may have experienced the same phenomenon while driving a car, while in the shower, or while listening to music. You may have experienced this situation just before going to sleep, or at the moment you woke up. At such moments you are in direct contact with the right side of your brain. Thoughts that had previously been unconscious become vividly clear, logically understood for the first time.

Dreams

When interpreting dreams, psychoanalysts are initially more interested in the emotional experiences that can be recalled by the dreamer, rather than the dream images themselves. They know that as a rule, dreams are nonverbal, emotional, and imaginative experiences, where time and logic have little meaning.

Dream images are transient. It is not clear if they are accurately recalled at all. At times, we seem to remember a dream, even if it is only for a short period. We all know that in order to increase our chances of remembering a dream, we must repeat it aloud to ourselves after waking up. In this way, the product of the right side of our brain can be registered in the left side of the brain, where the center of speech is located. It is easier to recall a dream once it has been written down in a diary or "night book". In order to be most successful in recalling and understanding a dream, we must remember that emotional experiences are the keys to the dream.

Research dealing with sleep and dreaming will probably be increased in the years to come. As we spend an average of twenty-five years of our life in bed, such research is quite justified. As many as six years during our lifetime may be spent involved in our dreams. In addition, we spend a considerable amount of our time day-dreaming. Whether we are jogging or driving a car, our thoughts wander as they may when we are dreaming. If at such times you happen to think of a good idea, we shall soon discuss a technique that you can use that will allow you to increase your chances of remembering, and ultimately benefitting from it.

Your subconscious mind

Our conscious thoughts make up only a small part of what goes on in our brain. Most of our thoughts take place on subconscious levels. One of Freud's greatest contributions was to discover that unconscious and preconscious thoughts are of vital importance to understanding human behavior. We will refer to these thoughts by their popular name, "subconscious thinking", throughout this book.

Under favorable conditions, bubbles from the subconscious can reach our conscious mind and be recognized by us. Many great ideas can emerge into our thoughts as a result of bubbles from the subconscious. The ideas often seem to come right out of the blue when they are least expected or sought after. Thoughts below your level of consciousness are continuously involved and affecting the known and unknown goals of your life, suggesting activities and solutions which could very well suit your needs.

Thoughts are like bubbles

If you work too hard too often, it becomes very difficult to achieve really good results. To a great extent, this is because you will not have the opportunities you need to experience the quiet and relaxing moments in which creative bubbles of thought can enter into your conscious mind. By working at a more relaxed tempo, and learning how to use the creative thoughts that can come to you under such conditions, you can achieve better results in less time than you were able to achieve beforehand.

Many examples can be cited to demonstrate this. I can recall a situation I was involved in some time ago. One Friday afternoon I was working on some accounts. I was disturbed over a difference of 72 dollars between debit and credit. Although I continued to examine the figures for two hours, I was unable to find the error. In the evening after entering my bed, I called upon my subconscious thoughts to help me solve the problem during the night. When I woke up in the morning, the numbers 91 and 19 were bubbling in my mind. After a while, I put the numbers in order and realized that the difference between 91 and 19 was 72. My subconscious thoughts solved the problem. By mistake, I had reversed the numbers 9 and 1, and had written 91 instead of 19.

When I arrived at my office, I found that I had written 591 instead of 519. In spite of checking my calculations several times, I was unable to find the error the night before. Only after I had gone to bed was my subconscious able to share with me the fault that had registered with it. My frantic adding activities on my calculator had hampered my subconscious from communicating the mistake. Had I paused and relaxed, I might have realized where to find the error that evening. I had begun to realize that the more relaxed you are when you work, the greater the opportunity your subconscious thinking has to be heard.

One thing at a time

We have mentioned how our mind can be limited by the way in which ideas can slip from it. Our subconscious thoughts can give birth to creative alternatives, which can just as easily be lost to us if they are not registered by the left side of our brain.

Another limitation of our mind is that we can only think about one thing during any given moment. It is not uncommon while working on something that we are very involved in, to pay too little attention to other things we ought to be paying attention to. When we are very involved in our work we may, for example, forget to telephone someone we had promised to call at that time. These limitations are restricting. It is good to know that the tools that you receive from this book will remove some of these limitations, and open up new possibilities for you.

The brain is not a computer

Although the human brain is often compared to a computer, the differences in the ways each work are so fundamental that this metaphor is ridiculous. A computer works in linear sequences from a given program; most often, the brain functions in parallel and holistic patterns. Human thoughts will wonder in various ways if they are not consciously and specifically directed.

Experimental studies support a holistic concept of memory. Studies have shown that when a mouse is taught to run in a certain direction in order to collect food, and when larger and larger parts of its brain are then surgically removed, a tiny part of its brain is all that is necessary to guide the mouse to its goal. This indicates that the information which was earlier put into the brain of the mouse was not restricted to a single area, but was distributed widely throughout its brain.

More ripples in water

The ability of the brain to work in a holistic way can be illustrated by another example. If two stones are thrown into the water, ripples are formed on the surface of the water. If these ripples could be frozen in time, a beautiful pattern of two systems of ripples, one interwoven into the other would appear. Every square inch of the frozen area would contain all of the information needed to find the spots where the stones landed. It wouldn't matter where in the area we cut out this square inch. We could form a whole picture from every tiny part.

Don't drown in the flood

A computer program gives a computer specific commands to carry out given tasks. The human brain receives no such programming. The brain receives information through its thoughts and from the environment that surrounds it, including telephone calls, company policies, and directions from supervisors. We are often the victims of a shower of impulses coming from many directions. It is no wonder that we have difficulties in achieving goal-oriented and rational ways of working.

One of the best ways of achieving a systematic way of working is to make use of the tools we are now ready to explore. If you are concerned that by using these tools you will become more like a computer or a robot, you are completely wrong. On the contrary, these tools can help you to have a freer and more pleasant life, with greater room for spontaneous experiences.

How spontaneous can a person be when drowning in a flood of impulses from unsolved problems in life, fighting to get to the surface?

You will use your insight

We have given a lot of time to exploring the workings of our brain. Our guiding impulses come from our brain. It is clearly to our advantage to obtain some insight into how the most important tool we have works. We are now in a better position to know ourselves, and to understand the thoughts behind our daydreams. You will have a better understanding about why simple tools can lead to very successful results. Our final goal is to work less by working smarter. By doing so, work will become more interesting and productive. Today can really be the first day in which you are in charge of the rest of your life. If you are dissatisfied with any area of your life, you now have a perfect opportunity to change it.

Go for it!

3 The simple and effective mind map

The mind map - a tool for many purposes

We shall now explore the mind map. The mind map is an exciting and efficient tool that can be applied to many jobs. It is particularly effective as a tool for improving your presentation skills for meetings and seminars. Being a more confident and interesting speaker can have a significant impact on your personal position.

The mind map is also a useful tool for you as a listener. It is a very helpful note taking device. It reduces your need to write to a minimum, and makes your notes more lucid and easy to understand. The notation techniques that we have been taught to use do not allow us to use our brain as fully as we would like. Most notation techniques make use of the logical capacities of the left side of the brain. The creative capacities of the right side of our brain are not often called upon during this process.

The mind map can also help you think more clearly. It is a useful problem solving tool. It allows you to have a better grasp of the entire problem, making it easier for you to find alternative and appropriate solutions. The mind map can help you develop and activate your plans more quickly. By making better use of your creative resources, the quality of your planning abilities will also increase.

To sum up, the mind map can help you in any activity that can benefit from creative thought. Whether you are developing a project, solving a problem. or writing a book, things will work out better, more simply, and more easily if you use this tool. In addition, mind maps are fun to use. Your work will be more enjoyable, which will motivate you to get started with it. As we have said before, we practice what we preach. The chapters of this book have been developed through mind maps.

The mind map is in tune with the brain

The mind map was first developed by the English author Tony Buzan. The mind map in the illustration on page 45 was developed by a student who was assigned to give a presentation about Florida. As you can see, it resembles the doodling or scribbling we do when we make phone calls. It takes advantage of the brain's natural ability to organize and to understand information. By following the way the brain works, the mind map gives this student an overall picture of what she is going to talk about. It also gives her a stronger and clearer understanding of the link between the subject titles of her presentation. It frees the presenter from being forced to treat the subject titles in any specific order. The flow from one part of a presentation to another can now be determined by immediate audience interaction, rather than by having to rigidly follow a text in a predetermined order.

The mind map is designed to give you greater control of your subject material. Your creative energies are stimulated when you develop a mind map. You will benefit from making new associations between ideas you are working with. As you continue to use mind maps, such ideas will develop rapidly, and on a regular basis.

Find the right words!

Speakers often rely on written text to help them with their lectures. By doing so, they feel less anxious about forgetting the ideas they would like to get across. Professional speakers know that such aids have a number of drawbacks. The use of written text may make the presentation boring and lifeless. Monotonous

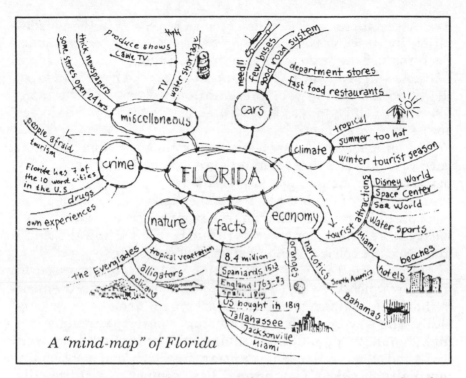

A "mind-map" of Florida

presentations put audiences to sleep. To compensate for this problem, experienced lecturers will divide their written aids in half. The best way is to place a mind map summarizing the content of the presentation on the left side of the lectern, and the complete text for the presentation on the right. By using this method, the presentation is certain to be more lively. Tony Buzan refers to "key words" as words that summarize the points on which a lecture is made. We prefer to say that the mind map is designed according to the principle of "summary points".

Let's take another look at the illustration above. The title of the presentation is written in the center of the mind map. To read the mind map, begin on the far right of the map, and continue in a counter clock-wise direction. The developer of this map has chosen to illustrate specific parts of the smaller circles. Coils that have been marked with key words in capital letters, have been used to emphasize specific aspects of the presentation.

Use your creative skills when you are developing a mind map. You may use colors or three-dimensional effects whenever you choose to. Figures and pictures should be used as often as you

45

like. Associations can be made between any parts of the presentation by drawing connecting arrows or shaded backgrounds. Feel free to exaggerate, use your sense of humor, or use bizarre concepts wherever you feel it is appropriate. The more you do so, the more interesting your presentation will be, and the more likely you will be to recall all of the ideas you would like to get across to your audience.

The mind map has other benefits as well. More often than not, once you have completed a mind map, you no longer need it. By using pictures, figures, and key words, you utilize the capacity of the right side of the brain to remember images. The capacity of your brain for remembering images is much greater than its capacity to remember ordinary written text. By using the mind map we can exploit a greater capacity of our brain.

Once people begin using mind maps, they are surprised to find how much their presentations improve. This improvement is due to benefits of the mind map beyond memory increasing skills. The way in which the mind map is developed results in a higher quality presentation than could be achieved without using the creative, amusing, exciting, intuitive, and emotionally moving right side of your brain. These components are equally important when utilizing the mind map as a problem-solving tool.

Teach this technique to your children

Teach your children to use a mind map. It is a very useful tool for them to have. It can be helpful, for example, when they show a lack of interest in their homework. Working on a project that is repetitive or that teaches them little is a very uninspiring experience. At such times sit down with your children. Write the name of the subject that has been assigned to them on a piece of paper, and draw a circle around it. Then draw key words, funny pictures, coils, and other interesting marks on the paper to illustrate the content of their assignment. You and your children will be pleased with the results of your efforts. By sparking an interest in your children to complete their assignment, they will have the energy to complete it in less time than it would have otherwise taken.

4 Bill and Alan - which one are you like?

True to life

What we are about to discuss is of course true. Bill and Alan exist in real life. Even if you have not met them, you will recognize their brothers and sisters.

Bill

Bill is 46 years old. He is the office manager of a scientific instruments company. He is convinced that his job as a manager has grown more and more complicated, primarily because of new policies, guidelines, government regulations, rules, and laws. He spends a good deal of time complaining about this subject to anyone who will listen. Currently, he is particularly dissatisfied with a policy regarding the choice of vacation days. Even though the policy has been in effect for several years, he has not had the time to read it. This has resulted in disagreements and problems with the other eighteen employees in the company. On several occasions, Bill has been assigned to management programs to help him develop his skills, but before he could attend the programs, more important things always seemed to turn up. Just recently he had to withdraw from a program because of a problem he was having with the ABC accounts.

Bill often feels tired. This is especially true when he sits in his office chair. His desk is covered with papers, which he finds exhausting to look at. But today, he has decided he will bring some order to his work. The last time he had decided that he needed order was last Monday. The first time he had decided that his desk needed to be put in order was on a Wednesday, twelve years ago. This time, he announces to himself, he will follow through with what has to be done.

Bill spends the first hour looking over his papers, without being able to get started. It occurs to him that a cup of coffee may help him get going. Although it is a short distance to the coffee pot, it takes him a long time to get there. In order to maintain a pleasant atmosphere in the office, he stops and talks with everyone that he meets. Bill has heard that it is important to have a good relationships at work. Sometimes, when he enters the offices of his associates, he gets the impression that they seem somewhat annoyed. He can't understand why that should be. Maybe, he reasons, his associates do not understand the importance of good working relationships.

After his coffee-break, he has one hour left before lunch time. Bill decides to strain every nerve to get something done, because soon half of his work-day will be gone. He frantically searches for a note he had written yesterday listing all of the things he was to take care of today. He can't remember where he put it. Bill is very worried that important notes on that piece of paper may be lost.

After lunch, Bill tries to get started with the budget for next year, but he is interrupted by telephone calls and a micro-computer salesman. He thinks that an office computer would solve his problems, and he would then have enough time to get his papers in order. He phones the sales representatives of five different companies in order to have a chat with each of them.

This salesman leaves at 5 PM. It is time for Bill to put papers in his briefcase. He must take them home, because he intends to spend his evening catching up on his work. His briefcase is full when he puts it down in his living-room. He remembers to call his neighbor to call off a tennis game he had planned to have at 6 PM. The neighbor regrets that the game has to be cancelled, but he understands that Bill has important work to do. On the other hand, he can't understand why Bill cancels appointments so often.

Bill's wife has prepared a special dinner to celebrate their twentieth anniversary. But is already half past seven, so Bill rushes through dinner in order to work on the papers he has taken home. He doesn't even have time to help Thomas, his oldest son, with his homework as he had promised. With a good grip on his briefcase, he strides along to his study, but on the way there his attention is caught by the evening news which is blasting from the television. He listens for the headlines. The last report is about a bankrupt company in a nearby city. He wonders what influence this might have on his own company, as he sits down in his armchair. Following the early news is a program about how smart businessmen avoid taxes. Naturally, he must see that program. It is now nine o'clock, and Bill gets out of his armchair, only to change the channels for a special news report.

Refreshed by a cup of coffee and a sandwich, Bill is finally sitting at his desk. As he opens his briefcase, he looks at his watch. It is now 10 o'clock. His mouth opens into a wide yawn. Just then, he realizes what must be done. He must go to bed at once, so that he can get up two hours earlier the next morning, when he feels refreshed and able to get through his work in peace and quiet.

Bill's wife has already gone to bed, and she is delighted when Bill arrives. She is hoping for a romantic end to their anniversary, which is why she has served sparkling wine. But Bill drank very little that evening because he knew that he would have to work. At least he is in the bedroom with her. But he just puts his briefcase on his bedside table, wishes her good night, and falls asleep.

At five o'clock the next morning, Bill is reminded by the ringing alarm clock that it is a new working day. Bill ordinarily gets up at seven o'clock, so he thinks that he can rest in bed for another minute or two. He turns off the alarm, so that it doesn't wake his wife, and promptly falls back to sleep.

Bill's wife shakes him awake at half past eight. Since he is due at work at eight o'clock, he skips breakfast, runs to his car, and speeds off to his office, where a computer salesman has been waiting for him for fifteen minutes. Before Bill meets him, he calls his wife to ask her to take a taxi to his office with the brief-case he had left in the bedroom.

Alan

Alan is 52 years old. He employs six people in his own accounting firm. He thinks that his staff is large enough, and does not wish to hire additional people. He has therefore developed a policy of not accepting a new client unless that client is more profitable to him than any client he already has. At that point, he finds another appropriate firm for the old client, so as to increase his profit without taking on more accounts. He is convinced that his policy works to the advantage of the clients that remain with him as well.

Alan does not like getting up early in the morning, so his agency does not open up until nine AM. His staff is not expected to work more than seven hours a day, although their salaries are equal to those of workers who are employed eight hours a day. To date, nobody has complained about this.

After saying good morning to his employees, Alan goes to his office and starts to work. He sets aside two undisturbed hours every day for planning and other jobs of vital importance. Yesterday , he worked with the accountant of his most important client on some tax problems that had resulted from an inappropriate recording system. Today, his first undisturbed hour will be spent designing a form to prevent the problem he worked on yesterday from occurring again. Alan believes that well designed forms can make difficult matters easier to handle. He has found that they save time, and can be used to prevent fires that would otherwise come up again.

Tomorrow it is Friday, and the office will be closed. Alan is leaving for Washington to attend a business conference with his staff. They will be gone for two days, and when they return home they will see a show and have dinner together. It has become their tradition to travel to a conference together once a year. This year they will learn about micro-computers. Up to now, they have been using a manual system in the office. The system they have been using is flexible and easy to handle. Balance sheets are completed quickly, and reports and final accounts have been dealt with by using standard forms. But Alan has been impressed with some articles he has read about applications of new technologies, so he and his staff will explore the advantages and disadvantages of owning their own microcomputer.

After designing a new form for estimating taxation, he empties the mail-box outside his door, where his employees can put notes and phone messages for his attention without disturbing him during his first two working hours. His door is of course always open for important messages and visitors.

The atmosphere in the office is relaxed and secure. A casual observer might conclude that the work performed must be boring. Staff members are satisfied. They appreciate the decentralized work structure. They work independently. Their good working relationships have been strengthened during the trips they have had together, and over lunch in different restaurants.

Alan leaves for home at four PM almost every day. As his wife works full time, it is his turn to pick up his youngest son from the baby sitter. He then prepares dinner for the family. He and junior heat the previously prepared meal they took from the freezer earlier that morning.

After dinner, Alan learns French in a study group that he attends twice a week. He has found that studying French helps balance the numerical work he spends so much time on during the day. One of Alan's secrets is that every now and again at work, he browses through French grammar books and dictionaries. Next summer his family will travel to the south of France, where they have reserved a cottage for two weeks. Alan will rent a small sailing boat there, similar to the one he and his oldest daughter built in their basement. This will fulfill his wife's dream of sailing in the Mediterranean, although she may have dreamt of a somewhat bigger boat.

At this point, we will let Alan and Bill continue their lives. But some questions need to be answered. Which of them has the greatest freedom? Will Bill ever clean up his desk? What advice would you like to give Alan? Can a human being be so perfect? Does Alan try to get his work done with as little effort as possible because he really doesn't like work?

Stay tuned for the next chapter for the answers to these questions.

5   How do you work?

Potential for improvement
We all have our own style of working. Of course we cannot guess
what your style of working is. It is probably somewhere between
the two extremes of Bill and Alan. We can also assume that you
are not completely satisfied with your current way of working.
But do not despair. Your potential for improvement is enormous!

Parkinson's law
Some great laws have been named after Parkinson. One law
states that any job will expand to fill all of the available time
that you give for it. This law applies to anyone you give a job to,
including yourself. Whether you give yourself half an hour or
several hours to do a job, you will keep busy during the time you
have set aside to do it. That's why you rarely see people twid-
dling their thumbs. No matter how little work people actually do,
they keep busy. Bill, for example, probably gives the impression
of being a hardworking and energetic man, although he accomplishes very little. He may also give the impression that he finds
it difficult to accomplish his work during normal working days.

Misplaced information is harmful to your health

When we are busily and vigorously engaged in a project, we are usually involved in correcting our own mistakes. If we were able to make correct decisions in the first place, we could be using our energies in far more enjoyable ways.

When we look at the way people work, we can spot certain patterns and distinguishing features about their particular work style. For example, we may often find people involved in the act of looking for something. They may be looking for specific information that they need to start or finish a job. Searching for information takes time, and can cause problems which may lead to in creased stress and fatigue. If you have been a victim of this type of situation, you can imagine the value of a system that will consistently give you quick and accurate access to the different kinds of information you need when you work. Such systems are seldom seen. When they could be most appreciate, they are most difficult to develop. At such times, you are so annoyed about not being able to find what you need that you have little energy left to sit down and plan preventive actions for future occasions.

Before you can develop an effective system for organizing your resources, you must regain control of your feelings and your thoughts. Once you do this, you begin to realize that without easy access to the information you require, you will not be able to make appropriate decisions that can affect your life, and the lives of those you care about. At such times, you recognize that your need for a more successful system of working is critical. You understand the importance of using the tools described in this book to put your life together as you want it to be.

Urgent jobs get in the way of important jobs

We often hear complaints about not having enough time to complete a job that has to be done. Needless to say, it is often the more important jobs that are not completed the way they should be. Important jobs are often put aside for urgent jobs, which managers tend to take on first. The problem is that urgent jobs are seldom very important, and important jobs are seldom urgent. As a result, important jobs are very often put aside for less important but urgent jobs. After some time, important jobs turn into urgent ones. At that point, there is little time to do the job right. A crisis will arise, and once again you will mutter to yourself that there must be a better way to work.

Nobody enjoys being in the situation where they must complete an important job without enough time to do it right. One goal of this book is to show you a way to work in which important jobs are completed first. Once you have achieved this skill, you will be amazed at how different you will feel as a result of having more control over your work life.

Our friend Bill was unable to create a situation in which he could work quietly and undisturbed. Unnecessary telephone calls and visitors can make your office a terrible place to work, at least during regular working hours. You may try to solve this situation by doing your work outside of regular business hours. When planning such activities, it is important to take into consideration the people and aspects in your life that you value. Ask yourself how taking action on one aspect will affect other aspects of your personal life as well as your work life.

The less extra time you need to do your work, the more time you will have for other things in your life, Let us work together to help you achieve a more efficient way of working, so that you may better enjoy the life you are working for.

Choose the job you want to do

As we have said before, don't bother planning you time. Instead, devote your energy to choosing what you would like to do during the time that you have available. Time goes on, uninfluenced by any of us. The only thing we can influence is the way we choose to use our time. Wise men and women spend their time on jobs that enable them to get the results they wish to achieve. For example, if you decide to live half of each year in Florida and half in New York, you must plan to achieve the goals that make this possible. Once you achieve the goals that you work for, your bonus will be feeling a tremendous sense of success.

In the next chapter, you will be introduced to a Model For Success that has been proven very successful for many people in many countries. The model will help you determine which jobs to give top priority to in order to reach your goals, and how you can get high priority jobs completed in a most satisfactory way.

6   The model for success - a useful test

The model for success

It would be impossible to learn how to bowl if we were never allowed to see or to hear the number of pins we knocked down after any try. In the same way, it is impossible to become more effective in our work life without being able to determine how effective we are as a result of trying new approaches. In this chapter, we shall learn to determine how effective our current pattern of work is, and how we can recognize when another style of work is more effective for reaching our goals. The tool we shall use is called The Model For Success.

The Model For Success is designed to make us more effective rather than more efficient in our work life. An efficient worker knows how to get a job done. An effective worker knows how to get the right job done. An important key for better life management is knowing when we are merely being efficient rather than effective in our daily routines. It is equally important for us to be able to know how well we perform and manage the jobs that we do take on.

The graph on page 57 containing two axes and a curve illustrates the model. The vertical axis helps us keep track of how successful we are at choosing the right kinds of tasks to work on. The higher we can place ourselves on this axis, the better we are at choosing the right kinds of tasks to take on. The horizontal

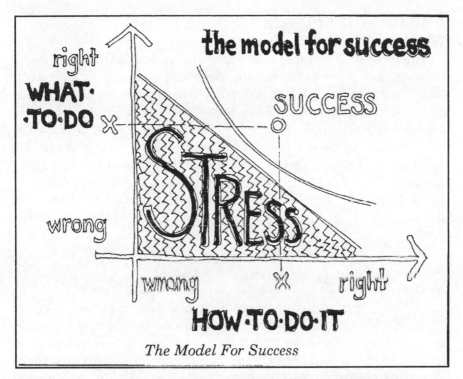

The Model For Success

axis of this model keeps track of how well we perform a task in the right way. The further to the right we can place ourselves on this axis, the better we are at managing our work life.

What the model does for you

We have two reasons for introducing the Model For Success to you at this time. One reason is that it identifies the basic components that success is made of. The second reason is that it helps us to understand the relationship between these components in achieving success.

If we are to manage our lives successfully, it is necessary for us to perform the right tasks in correct ways. In the sections that follow, you will discover how to achieve what you want by first climbing up the horizontal WHAT-TO-DO-axis, and then by advancing to the right along the vertical HOW-TO-DO-IT-axis.

Locate Bill and Alan

Where do Bill and Alan fit in this model?

Alan knows a number of things that he wants from life. As he is described, Alan performs the right tasks in practically faultless ways. He does not allow himself to become so absorbed by any one task that he is unable to see the forest for the trees. He successfully accomplishes what he wants to achieve. Bill, on the other hand, performs the wrong tasks in the wrong ways. He loses sight of his goals when he is confronted by anything along his path. He would like to find his way out of the forest, but he is not sure about where he should go, or how he can get there. Do not despair. If Bill reads this book, he will be able to reach his goals.

What's what?

As we have stated before, most people do not often work on the right kinds of tasks because they get side-tracked by more urgent, but less important tasks. It is not easy to overcome our nature to seek out and perform routine jobs before important tasks requiring planning. We get a feeling of satisfaction from completing a task, regardless of how unimportant the job may be. The completion of a routine task can often provide us with a feeling of immediate gratification.

Herbert Simon, a Nobel prize winning economist, observed that people tend to avoid uncertainty in decision making. When we take responsibility to perform important jobs, we often experience moments of uncertainty. We may think "Do I have what it takes to accomplish this task? Can I really pull this off?" Such moments of uncertainty can keep us from even starting an important task. Psychologists link these moments to the fear of success, and to the fear of failure. To be successful we must strive to challenge the uncertainty we experience within ourselves. As we discover that we can win battles against our own uncertainties, it will become increasingly easy to enter them.

Let's stop for a moment and think about the WHAT-TO-DO-axis. How effective are you at choosing your tasks? Do you choose them at random? Do you tend to take on tasks that lead to success and to a life that you enjoy? There is a little test that can help you determine how well you choose tasks that lead to success. Take a pencil and put a mark on the WHAT-TO-DO-axis at the point that corresponds to the approximate percent of time you work on the right kinds of tasks during a typical working day. If you believe that you do not have time to work on important tasks on a daily basis, your mark will appear towards the lowest end of the axis. If you believe that you usually choose to work on the right kinds of tasks, your mark will appear towards the high end of this axis.

Where are we now?

As you did on the WHAT-TO-DO-axis, estimate the point on the HOW-TO-DO-IT-axis that indicates how successful you generally are at accomplishing the tasks you take on in your daily routines. Mark that point in pencil. Draw a perpendicular line from that point into the chart, to meet a perpendicular line drawn from the point you have chosen on the WHAT-TO-DO-axis. Compare the size of the area within these boundaries to the total size between the two axes. The area you have drawn represents how successful you currently consider yourself to be compared to how successful you could be.

This area you have marked off reflects your current position on this chart. It is only your starting point on your road to successful life management. As you read this book, and learn how to use the tools it puts at your disposal, the amount of space representing success on this chart will grow significantly. Soon, we will ask you to estimate your position on this chart again. At that time, a comparison of your two charts should prove to be an eye opening experience.

What about how?

It is obvious that knowledge and experience are required for us to perform a job well. It is less obvious that certain tools can help us capitalize on our knowledge and experience in order to perform a job even better. These tools help to motivate and energize us, maximize our planning and problem solving skills, provide us with the resources that we need, and encourage us to reap the benefits of our efforts.

Before you can perform a job well, you must be able to get started with it. This is often easier said than done. With this in mind, we have developed some methods to help you get started on important jobs easily and quickly. These methods are particularly effective for getting you started on important tasks. As we have defined them, important tasks are those that rarely need immediate attention, but turn out to be most beneficial for you the sooner they are completed.

We have already introduced one tool that can help you advance in the right direction along the HOW-TO-DO-IT-axis. It is the mind map. Using the mind map increases your motivation and interest in your job. Because the mind map is fun to use, it is easy to get started on it. Because the mind map stimulates and encourages creative thought, it helps you accomplish the tasks you work on in a more effective way.

It is rarely a good idea to use inferior material when manufacturing a product. In the same way, it is not a good idea to make decisions based on insufficient or inaccurate information. If we want to achieve good results from our labors, we must have methods for obtaining the information we need quickly and effectively. These methods should be useful for dealing with the documents and information that are a part of our personal life as well as our work life.

The environment

Our discussion on the Model For Success would be incomplete if we did not include some words about the environment in which we work. What you choose to work on, and how you choose to do it is influenced by the environment in which you are working. You may understand both what it is that you are to do, and how you are to do it. But your work-environment might be so detrimental to your work that it suppresses your appetite for work, and effects your results. Consider the situation of a teacher who is assigned to work with an impossible class. The students enter their classroom after the bell has rung. They scatter around the room, talking among themselves and provoking the teacher. Although this teacher may be very able to educate normal students, the teacher's ambition is completely suppressed by the disruptive behavior of bad pupils.

It is unfortunate if your working environment does not allow you the time you need to work on important tasks. In many situations, interruptions are a normal part of the job that workers must learn to adjust to. For instance, if you were a manager in a bank, you would have to serve the needs of your clients as they appear. In such situations, you may have to adjust the time you work on important tasks to coincide with the hours that customers are not allowed in the bank. On the other hand, most disturbances are unnecessary. You may be interrupted by colleagues who lack the discipline to do their work without disturbing others. They may find you to be a good listener to be taken advantage of any time, if you lack the courage to turn them away.

Your environment is also a product of the structure of the organization you are a part of. Your relationship with the people you work with, the clarity of goals within your organization, and the methods used to motivate and inspire employees will effect your work. In the chapters ahead, you will discover how you can modify the effects of many of these factors. In addition, Chapters 12 and 13 review some of the things you can do to improve your work environment.

The model and your conscious thoughts

We will enlarge the area of success that you have plotted in your Model For Success by increasing your skills to choose the right kinds of tasks, to perform those tasks well, and to improve your work environment. We can reach these goals by using the simple tools we present. By now you are aware that it is necessary to change some bad habits you have acquired over the years in order to succeed in managing your life better. Your level of consciousness is now tuned to learning how to use the tools that will help you to achieve your goals.

Let's move on!

Part B

What we can do

What can we do?

Before we can determine the best way to do something, we must first decide what we should work on. We will begin this section by examining the WHAT-TO-DO-axis on the Model For Success.

Don't be obsessed by pay day!

How do you determine which jobs to do? How do you set your priorities? Do you have a work pattern?

If you are like most people, you may feel as if chance is responsible for determining the jobs you do. With few exceptions, your assignments may be coming from telephone calls, orders, work delegated from other levels, visits, memos, and other outside sources, rather than your own determination.

If you do not set priorities for yourself, it is not surprising that you are often short of time. You will find yourself buried in the urgent job requests of other people. Because urgent jobs demand immediate attention, you will tend to give the urgent job requests of others priority over your own important work.

As you will recall, important tasks are seldom urgent. Management activities such as developing staff, solving problems, making important business arrangements, and enforcing policies do not have to be made on any particular business day. Consequently, it is easy to postpone important tasks. But sooner or later, the need to take care of important tasks will become urgent. You will feel as anxious as if you had a knife held at your throat. Once you no longer have the time to carry out an important task, you will find yourself at the beginning of a crisis that may not be easy to resolve. At such times, a number of things may go wrong. You may not be able to get hold of the people and resources that you need. Mistakes or misunderstandings may lead to poor decisions that cannot be identified or corrected in moments of crisis. Even worse, you may find that an entire job must be redone, with even less time to do it properly. This could lead to an even greater crisis.

This pattern of losing control can be broken by using the tools in this book to work more effectively. If you follow our advice, you will learn to recognize the jobs that you should do from those that cannot carry you very far. You can surf on waves of success, instead of "wiping out" on unimportant activities that require your immediate attention.

7　Spend pennies for your thoughts

Capture your dreams

Let's begin with a management tool that can help you reduce stress, and increase your determination. This tool is a simple notebook. You can understand the importance of this tool when you consider how it can be used to help use your brain to better advantage.

As you will recall, the brain is continually working. Most of our thinking occurs on a subconscious level. Thoughts emerge from this level and then fall back into it. Many of these thoughts are very useful for decision making and problem solving. But these thoughts are as lucid as our dreams, and must be written down as quickly as possible if they are to be remembered. The helpful ideas emerging from the creative hemisphere of the right side of our brain will soon be forgotten if we do not have a system to capture them. The best system is to be prepared to write them down as soon as they occur.

At the first chance you have, get a notebook that can be easily available to you at all times. It should be so small that you will not mind keeping it in your pocket wherever you go. As we have discovered, we are most creative when we are engaged in somewhat odd activities, such as running or playing. At such times, having a notebook available allows us to exploit this creativity. As silly as it may seem, have your notebook available to you the

Use your creative abilities

next time you go jogging. Place the notebook on your bedside table before you go to sleep, so that you can take advantage of the creative moments that occur just before falling to sleep, or as you awaken. You will discover that the thoughts that you record will be useful to you now as well as in the future.

When you are showering

Everyone has their own unique time when they are most creative. You will soon discover the circumstances in which you are most creatively productive. You may find that while you are showering in the morning, you think of three or four things you would like to take care of during the day. By the time you are having your breakfast, you can remember only one of the thoughts. If you use a notebook, you will be more willing to record your thoughts immediately after showering.

You can't say that it's too difficult

A notebook is an important management tool. It allows you to record an important thought as rapidly as you think it. You do not have to write neatly, and you do not have to organize your thoughts in any special way. Personal matters and work matters can be mixed together in whatever way you choose. You can record telephone numbers, presentation ideas, jokes, project outlines, addresses, items you need to buy, recipes, trip tips, people's names, journal references, transportation schedules, stock tips, or anything else you would like to remember. You can use your notebook as a kind of basic register, and transfer your notes elsewhere, as you see fit.

It is not too late to learn how to tap into your creative capacities. Begin with at least one notebook. It should be as thin and as easy to carry as possible. The less you carry it, the less access you will have to your normally subconscious creative thoughts.

You must realize that your subconscious thoughts are success oriented. They work to resolve the conflicts and stress in your mind, including those resulting from unfulfilled goals, interests and needs. Subconscious thoughts are more honest than most conscious thoughts. They are less likely to be distorted by psychological defense mechanisms. Your notebook should serve not only as a tool for making more creative decisions, but more intelligent and honest decisions as well. You and your notebook can work effectively to utilize the great qualities of your brain, as well as to become less affected by restrictive thinking. Get yourself a notebook before you read any further, and carry it with you.

The missing notebook

During our management programs, we often ask participants if they use a notebook. Although many managers do use notebooks on a regular basis, not one participant has used a notebook as we have just described before the course. Calendars are commonly carried around by managers, but they have limited space for note writing, and are not as useful. The most useful tool you can buy in order to take advantage of your creative thoughts is a common, inexpensive, little notebook. After you have filled it with valuable ideas, get another one.

If you follow this suggestion, within a few weeks you will praise this simple inexpensive tool, and wonder why you had not thought of using it before. At such times, remember that you had not been able to appreciate the value of your subconscious thoughts as you can now.

One reason the notebook has received little publicity is because office supply companies cannot make much of a profit by selling such an inexpensive tool. Expensive electronic devices and computer systems often have huge advertising budgets behind them. They appeal to the many people who believe they can solve their problems by throwing money at them. In reality, a human brain supported by an inexpensive notebook is more effective for most managerial problem solving than any computer.

There are many advantages to recording your creative ideas in a notebook in addition to that of being able to remember them. The process of capturing creative thoughts will inspire and energize you. You will find it easier to get started on your work and to continue with it. You will have a greater appreciation for your own creative skills, and your ability to solve problems. You can thumb through the physical evidence within your notebook to marvel at the powers within you. As your interest in your subconscious thinking grows, you will become more skilled in using your notebook. It will prove to be helpful in both your personal life and your work life.

The techniques of recording one's thoughts on a regular basis is not entirely new. Artists, scientists, authors, and other great thinkers have used similar tools to capitalize on their creative thoughts. Leonardo Da Vinci would always review the creative thoughts he had during the day just before falling asleep. Ernst Rolf, a famous Swedish songwriter, always carried a notebook to record lyrics or melodies that came to him. In spite of his early death, he contributed to the creation of approximately 700 songs. One famous film director got his best ideas while in the high jumping pit of a sports arena. He would write his ideas down in the sand, and return with a paper and pencil to record them. Nowadays he carries a notebook.

The author of this book have used this tool for several years, and would find it hard not to use it. It is not uncommon to write an idea down on the way to work, and feel inspired by it throughout the day.

I was scared

Do not be alarmed if you should feel a bit unsettled when you begin to use your notebook. When we first begin to discover how beneficial our subconscious thoughts are, it may be a bit frightening. We may discover new dimensions of ourselves, which we had not been aware of before. Although we have all had clever ideas, we seldom pay any attention to the process that gave them to us. It is a bit unsettling to know that everyone has the gift of creativity, but only a few people know how to use it.

Within days after you begin to use your notebook, you will find that you do not want to do without it. It will help you avoid extra work and stress in many situations. You will take care of things more easily. Because it will help you have smoother running work days, you will have more spare time.

We have discussed how important a notebook can be for exploiting our subconscious thoughts and increasing our intellectual capacities. Your notebook is a useful tool for planning or taking notes. It can also be used to record a what-to-do-list, which is discussed later in this chapter.

In Bethlehem too

The notebook is a tool that will help you to identify WHAT-TO-DO. It will help you to profit from both conscious and subconscious thought processes. The subconscious is often involved with life goals that we usually do not verbalize. It is classically demonstrated in the well known story about Charles Schwab, the General Manager of Bethlehem Steel. Unsatisfied with his work style, he sought advice from a personal planning consultant. Schwab promised to pay the consultant according to what he thought the advice was worth. The consultant suggested that during the evening Schwab make a list of six things that he should do during the next day, and try to accomplish as many of these things as possible. He was told to make another list for the next evening, but keep the items that he had not yet finished if they were still relevant. He was to be sure to always have six things on his list.

Schwab was surprised by the excellent results he achieved by following the consultant's advice. This technique became an important tool he used to get his work done. He presented the idea to his employees, who also achieved excellent results for themselves and for their organization. The consultant was paid $25.000, which was quite a sum of money at the time.

The consultant's simple advice was successful because it forced Schwab and his employees to choose between important and less important work. They could not run away from the items on the lists in front of them. Without a visible list of important work, urgent and routine matters sooner or later take precedence. The list forced them to plan and prioritize their tasks. Schwab and his employees were forced to think about WHAT-TO-DO. The result was that they were more inclined to do what should be done.

This story clearly demonstrates that the main object of planning should be tasks, rather than time.

Becoming your own consultant

If you would like to follow the consultant's advice, you can record the things you would like to accomplish tomorrow in your notebook. A separate WHAT-TO-DO list may be used as well. Another advantage to keeping your WHAT-TO-DO list in your notebook is that you can use the other notes in your notebook as a reference for the items on your list. You will have full access to your thought bubbles. Your notebook with its WHAT-TO-DO list will be an effective tool which will give your work a new dimension.

Your notebook will allow you to be your own consultant. You don't have to limit your list to six items. Write down however many items you feel is appropriate. What is important is that the list forces you to stop and think before planning your work for the next day. It is important to realize that a few minutes of planning every evening can save you two hours of unnecessary work on an average day. That can add up to quite a lot of time for other activities during a year. In addition, you will find that your

WHAT-TO-DO list has other advantages as well, such as providing you with a system for having your work ready on time.

One variation of this tool is to keep a permanent WHAT-TO-DO list close to where you work. You can jot down whatever relates to what you have to do, regardless of how important or unimportant it is. Many time management consultants suggest that each items should be marked with an "A", "B", or "C", according to its importance. We find this procedure too complicated. Once you have chosen to do something, the next step is simply to get it done.

Begin with the most difficult job

If you are not sure which item should be selected first from your WHAT-TO-DO list, there are a number of things that you can do. You might decide to begin your work day by starting with an important, and preferably an unpleasant or boring task first. Once that job is out of the way, knowing that the worst is already over will help to brighten up the rest of your day.

If you decide to keep a master WHAT-TO-DO list close to where you work, it would not be surprising if it occasionally expands to contain 20 or 30 items that have yet to be taken care of. If you absolutely cannot make up your mind about which task should be completed next, one exciting way of tackling the list is to close your eyes and put a finger on any task on the list. Read it, and do it. Accept no excuses. Once the job is finished, you will feel both pleased and surprised as you cross it off the list.

The most difficult step

Once you have written down what has to be done, the probability of remembering what it is, and actually doing it is many times greater than if you had not done so. Even if you lose your notebook, the very act of recording what it is that you are to do will increase your chances of getting it done. The first step is always the hardest one to take, but once you have acknowledged in writing that you are going to begin it, you have taken that first step. Furthermore, once you develop a written concept about what you are going to do, your subconscious actively begins to work on it.

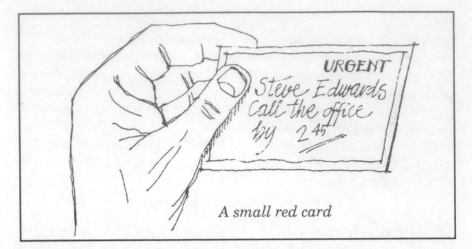

A small red card

If, for example, you write a note to remind yourself to buy bags for your vacuum cleaner, it would not be surprising if a thought bubble reminded you to buy them while passing a hardware store. If you had not made a note to yourself to buy the vacuum cleaner bags, it is unlikely that you would have thought to get them in the same situation.

The WHAT-TO-DO list can be applied to a variety of situations in your life. Wherever you use it, it will lead to excellent results.

A small red card

One limitation about being human is that we often forget to do what we had decided we would do. This limitation may get us into a variety of embarrassing situations. How many of us have been in a situation, for example, where we have received a telephone call requesting something which we promise to take care of at once, but soon after are sidetracked by another phone call, and do not think about responding to the first caller's needs until we are climbing into bed.

Not everyone can be entered on a WHAT-TO-DO list. One tool that can be helpful in such circumstances is a stack of small red index cards. Once you keep such cards close to where you work, you can jot down anything that requires your immediate attention on a note that cannot easily be misplaced. Leave it on your desk where it can be easily seen until it is resolved. Do not stack them up.

This is just one more simple tool to help you manage your life as you would like to manage it. If you use it in the right situations, it will help save you from awkward situations.

8 Your self starter is made out of paper

An important ingredient for success

Everyone who works has objectives to complete. If we are lucky, we may understand how our work objectives effect the organization. The more we understand why something must be done, the better we can do it. To understand what we must do, we need time to give it the thought it deserves.

Unfortunately, this seldom happens. Most people do not know what their goals are. They know even less about how their job fits into the scheme of things. Their assignements come from sources outside of themselves, including supervisors, clients, co-workers, and memos. It is unusual to take on a job as a result of one's own decision to do so. Because so much of the work day involves carrying out assignments from others, it is not surprising that so many workers are poorly motivated.

If we are to manage our lives well, we must realize that we are best motivated by our own ideas. Once we are motivated, we act. Once we see the fruits of our actions, we are encouraged to come up with new ideas. This circle of ideas, motivation, action, and reward is a major ingredient for success.

Another tool

At this time we shall introduce a new tool, called a Self Starter. The Self Starter is designed on the principle that generally, people do only what they are reminded to do. If you are interested in a particular activity, you will remind yourself to do it. If you are not interested in a particular activity, you must find some other way to remind yourself to do it so that it actually gets done. One way is to use a Self Starter.

The only materials you need are a piece of paper and a pencil. Write down some of the goals that you would really like to reach, but which for some reason you tend to ignore, on the piece of paper. Do not write down goals that are so obvious that there is no need to remind yourself of them. Try to recall goals that you would probably not attempt to complete if you were not reminded to do so.

Once you have completed the list, study it carefully. Keep it with you, so that you may carefully examine it several times during the week. The more often you look on the list, the less intimidated you will be by it. Every time you look at the list, ask yourself what you could do during the week to reach your goals. When you think of ideas, write them on your WHAT-TO-DO list.

When constructing a Self Starter, there are a number of things that you should consider. First, describe every goal you

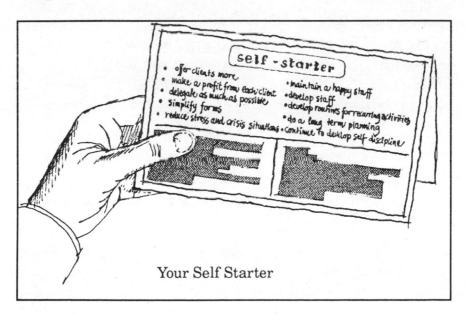

Your Self Starter

The Self Starter is built on the principle that:

You will only do what you are reminded of.

Comments: When you feel an interest and involvement in tasks that you are responsible for, you will automatically remind yourself to get them done. But other activities will get done only after you are reminded to begin them. These activities should be included in your Self Starter.

The Self Starter leads to:

A better match between your goals and your daily tasks.

Comments: Make a note of the goals you have a strong desire to reach, but for whatever reasons you have ignored. The more you see these goals when you review your Self Starter, the more likely you are to begin tasks which will bring you closer to achieving these goals

What the Self Starter includes:

The Self Starter includes goals which you would like to be more involved with.

Comments: Certain work goals are so obvious that you don't have to be reminded of them. Do not include them in your Self Starter.

write down as clearly and as concisely as you can. Sample goals may include: listening more, relaxing, or giving employees more effective feedback. Limit your list to six or seven items. Check to see that you are listing goals, rather than specific activities or jobs. If you are a manager, include technical, staff development, administrative, and personal activities. By including all of these

---

How do you use the Self Starter?

Study and think about your Self Starter several times a week (e.g. Friday afternoon, Monday morning and some other time). Ask yourself what you can do during the coming weeks in order to move closer to the goals you have identified. The results of your thoughts can be put into immediate action, or can be included in your notebook, in your WHAT-TO-DO list, or in your planning calender.

Comments: If you use this tool as we have described, you will be motivated to get started on the "right tasks", with actions following your thoughts. This simple approach will help you become more results oriented.

---

areas when arranging your goals, the risk of neglecting any managerial responsibilities is reduced. If your goals are stated too generally, they may become meaningless, and it may be hard to get concrete results from them. Do not neglect to examine your Self Starter several times each week. You can add to it whenever you wish.

Finally, do not be too concerned about violating any of the suggestions we have given for developing a Self Starter. If you do, it will be difficult to get started. A less than perfect Self Starter is much more valuable than none at all.

Your Self Starter will help you to think before you act. It will help you to be more effective by encouraging you to work on the right kinds of jobs.

Let's get started

Goals are neglected when you are not sure how to begin to achieve them. You may wonder, for example, how you can help create a more congenial atmosphere among your associates. As the ancient proverb states, the best way to eat an elephant is one bite at a time. Make a note to ask some of your associates out to lunch. Once you have accomplished this, add other ideas to your notebook. Before you realize what has happened, you will have accomplished a Self Starter goal.

Goal setting does not have to be boring

Personal planning programs often emphasize the importance of setting appropriate work goals for yourself. If that is all they do, the program will fail. You cannot develop work goals without giving equal consideration to the goals of your personal life.

Another problem with traditional personal planning programs is that you may be asked to set goals sequentially for the next two, five, and sometimes ten years. Demands such as these exhaust people as soon as they hear them. They make people squirm. People don't behave in such systematic, robot-like ways. More often than not, they don't want to be pressured into following such linear behavior sequences.

The Self Starter is a tool that allows you to determine your goals in a freer way. You are not restricted to linear associations between goals. You are free to focus in on goals which may not be connected to each other, but are important, and which you would otherwise tend to ignore. You can choose your goals as creatively as you care to. Goal setting does not have to be boring.

Fantastic results with inexpensive equipment

You can achieve significant control over your work by using an ordinary piece of paper and a pencil properly. Common sense and simple tools are much more effective than expensive planning calendars or electronic devices. The tools that we have described so far are so inexpensive and simple to use that it takes courage to discuss them. Our tools are so simple that it may be hard for individuals who are accustomed to complicated lives to realize how effective they are. The logic behind the techniques is sound, simple and refreshingly obvious. But logic is not the focus of these tools. What is important is that you use them to manage your life in a more effective way. This is not so easy to do, but you will succeed because of your interest in doing so.

Get started!

It is now time to spend some hours thinking about what you are aiming for in your work life. Even if you work for yourself, you may want to give this some thought. You can begin by writing down some goals that you would like to achieve in your job. Add these goals to your Self Starter list. It is as easy as that to begin a new and exciting work life for yourself.

It is up to you to create and explore new possibilities in your work life. If you let the days fly by and your work continues to be determined by forces outside of yourself choosing the things you must do, your chances of benefitting from new opportunities are small.

The Self Starter is a tool that can help you achieve what you want, and help you to feel good about yourself. The better you feel about yourself, the more relaxed you will be. The more relaxed you are, the more effectively you can work.

The marketing manager of a small ship yard

Suppose that you are the marketing manager of a small ship yard, and that you have decided to construct your first Self Starter. A marketing manager's job is often instructured. Success depends on one's ability to take initiatives. While thinking over your goals, you realize that one of them is to help develop the company's public image. Although you have done little to achieve this goal before, you have decided that you will begin to work towards it now. You write "Perform active Public Relations functions" in your Self Starter. After writing down this goal, you contact two trade journals, and invite them to your company to show them the organization's new production techniques. You set dates for the meetings and note them in your calender.

You then write "Export products" as a second goal in your Self Starter. You have not made much of an effort to do this before either. Domestic sales have been satisfactory, but you have suspected for some time that it would be worthwhile to explore export opportunities.

An exhibition in London

As you continue to use your Self Starter, you wonder if it is possible to reach another long time goal that you have had. You would like to attend the Earls Court Boat Show in London. You take out some paper and start to write a few notes. You call the exhibition organizers and collect some information regarding the costs of the conference, plane fares, and living arrangements. You are now moving towards your goal. It is true that you may have gotten started on this activity without the help of your Self Starter, but that may have been years in the future, rather than right now.

The training manager realizes his goal

Imagine that you are the manager of the training department of an organization. While working with your Self Starter, you realize that you have an important goal that you have been neglecting for a long time. You make a note in your Self Starter to explore a paricular training program for senior management. Later that week, as you review the goals you have written down, you feel an urge to get started on that activity, which you are convinced will work for the benefit of your company.

Before using your Self Starter, you could not always gather the energy to start new projects. Now you find yourself involved in planning a new project without really understanding how it happened. You begin by getting a list of programs that are offered to senior management by different organizations. You set up meetings with some senior managers to determine their interest in various topics. You determine a budget for the program, and decide how it would be justified and paid. You wonder to yourself why you waited so many years to act on this project. You had always known that it was important, but you had never realized how easy it was to start the project.

A tool for inspiration

The Self Starter inspires you to take on jobs to achieve the results you want. It offers an option to being a slave to the urgent but unimportant jobs of others for the rest of your life. You can finally get started on your important work. You do not have to wait to begin until there is enough time to properly complete what is important to you. Aside from the obvious advantages of having adequate time for important work, you will also gain from reducing the negative consequences of stress. The continuous satisfaction you will achieve as a result of being able to complete important goals will inspire you to continue along this road.

Alan's Self Starter

As you will recall from our comparison of Bill and Alan, Alan greatly values his personal life and his family. To him, working is a means of getting the resources that he needs to support his family and personal life style. One of his most important goals is to have his work day function as smoothly as possible, with a minimum amount of stress or side show activities. Alan finds his Self Starter to be an important tool to achieve his goals. It helps him plan his work in an organized way.

Alan's Self Starter	
• Offer clients more services	Technical goals
• Determine that each client is profitable to maintain	
• Delegate as much as possible	
• Simplify forms	
• Maintain a happy staff	Personnel related goals
• Develop staff	
• Develop routines for recurring activities	Administrative goals
• Continue to develop self-discipline	Self development goals

Alan knows that his Self Starter should include a variety of goals, so that he will not become too engrossed in any one area. Typically, his Self Starter will include technical, personnel related, administrative and self development goals as shown on the previous page.

It would be fantastic

You may be thinking, "It would be fantastic if all I have to do is to sit in my office and choose to work on whatever I felt was important, without having to worry about the demands others place on me. But my phone rings all day long, and people are always running in and out of my office."

If these are your concerns, our response is as follows. Many of the interruptions that pull your attention from your work may be the result of poor planning on your part in the first place. People may be running in and out of your office because the division of responsibilities between you and them may not be clear. Work may not be delegated as well as it could be. If you are willing to face questions such as these, you will discover some of the reasons why you feel that you are under great pressure so often. If you follow the advice within this book, you can eliminate many of the pressures which make you feel like a prisoner at work. You will feel more relaxed, and will have more time to enjoy life. As a result, your work routines will begin to improve, and you will be less disturbed by outside influences.

Some people are impressed by offices where the phones are constantly ringing, and where people are running from one place to another. The impression such offices may give of a dynamic company may be a false one. What really matters is the value of what is accomplished, not the amount of unnecessary energy used to achieve what is accomplished. By the same token, an office in which the atmosphere is quiet and relaxed is not necessarily an efficient one.

You do not have to acceept the assumption that as long s you work, you must live with continuous interruptions. You are responsible for how you get your work done. You decide the most effective way to respond to phone calls and visitors. The most difficult thing you need to achieve is to gather the confidence to make these decisions. We will come back to this point.

What is your personal life like?

As our discussion turns away from your work life and towards your personal life, we will not stop referring to the Self Starter. It is a useful tool for getting started towards all kinds of goals which might otherwise be put off. To illustrate this, let's return to the example of the marketing manager at the small ship yard.

As a child, this manager had not been exposed to music in his home. For some time he has been concerned that his own children would be as isolated from music as he was himself. He makes a note in his personal Self Starter to stimulate his children's musical talents. After taking this first step, he is inspired to look through the local newspaper to find concerts that he can take his children to over the weekend. As a result of taking the first simple step in his Self Starter, over the next two years, he and his family attended ten concerts. This is more than he had previously attended in his entire life. During this time, he also arranged for his children to have music lessons, which they enjoy.

Think about the goals that you would like to reach in your personal life. Note them in your Self Starter. Whether you would like to learn a foreign language, build up your body, improve your self-discipline, or plant a garden, you take your first step when you enter it into your Self Starter. As you think more about your goals, you may decide to eliminate those which have been driving you crazy for so many years, and are not realistic. If, for example, you had thought about learning to speak French, but now have other interests which make time for this activity imposible, eliminate it. You are better off spending a little time mourning the death of such goals, and putting them behind you. The sooner you discard unrealistic goals, the sooner you will free yourself from unwarranted guilt, and the more you will be able to begin the goals that would give you the greatest satisfaction to achieve.

Learn how to say "No"!

As we have seen, many demands are made on you to perform well at work and in your personal life. To survive these demands, you must learn to realistically choose those jobs which are most likely to lead to the results you want to achieve. You may be asked by your boss, for instance, to take on a job that you do not consider worth doing. More often than not, it is better to tell your boss your concerns about doing that job, than to blindly start it, and later have trouble completing it. If your reasons are valid, your boss might agree with you. If they are not, your boss might give you some insight as to why the job should be done.

Most of us say "No" to other adults so rarely, that we have to practice saying it until we are comfortable doing so. "No" is a powerful word for life management. It has the power to free us from some very distressing situations. Studies have demonstrated that people who can say "No" have fewer psychosomatic symptoms than people who can not. With practice, it becomes easier to say than you may imagine. Once you can say it in the appropriate ssituations, you will gain the respect of others as well as yourself.

With the help of your Self Starter, you will do it!

84

Part C

How we can do it

How we can do it

We will now look at a second component that will influence how successful you can be. This component will help you work in the most efficient ways on the activities that you have chosen to do. So far we have talked about how you can determine WHAT-TO-DO. You have learned how to use a number of tools to choose the right tasks to take on. We will now determine HOW-TO work on the projects you have chosen to do.

In reality there is no single right way or wrong way to complete a task. However some methods of working on tasks are more efficient than others. They yield greater results from less effort than other methods require. The horizontal line of the Model For Success is designed to show how efficient you are at accomplishing tasks. The further you move to the right of this axis, the more efficient you are at accomplishing your goals. It is not necessary to be perfect to be successful. You can achieve the success you would like by working in a fairly correct way on the goals you set out to achieve.

9 Simple tips for getting started

Get started!

No goal can be accomplished unless a first step is taken towards it. Taking a first step is not always easy. Consider what we can learn from the laws of physics. Before an object can be moved, a lot of energy is needed to overcome friction. Once an object is in motion, less energy is required to keep it moving. The laws of inertia also apply to the way we work. It takes great effort to overcome resistance and start a new activity. Once we begin to move forward, we are assisted by our starting speed.

People postpone work for many reasons. One common reason is that they lack the confidence that they can complete it as well as they would like to. Many good college students, for example, put off writing a term paper because they are afraid they are not ready to write a great term paper. When brought to an extreme, this fear can result in the student failing the course. Another reason is that by postponing a job long enough, people have an unconscious excuse for not having to do their work in a satisfactory way. We will not dwell any longer on the reasons why we have procrastinated in the past. It is more important that we look ahead, and provide ourselves with the right tools to overcome whatever resistance we may have to getting our jobs done effectively.

Urgent does not mean important

We have discussed in detail the relationship between important matters that are not always urgent, and urgent matters that often are not important. A job may be urgent only in the sense that it requires immediate attention. We have seen how easy it is to become enslaved under the tyranny of such urgent demands. A major goal of this book is to give you the tools you need to break away from the chains of urgent demands, and have the time that is necessary to work on important tasks.

You are not alone

Let's look at some tools that will help you to get started on your work. It is human nature to postpone whatever you can. The more important it is for you to do well on a job, the stronger is the tendency to postpone doing it. Psychologists have attempted many explanations for this phenomenon, including fear of failure and fear of success. When we postpone doing important tasks, we attempt to deal with the disappointment we feel about ourselves by choosing to do routine work or spinning our wheels. By trying to convince ourselves that routine work is useful, we attempt to silence our guilt and disappointment in ourselves. But a chronically guilty conscience will not go away. Sooner or later, we must complete the important work that has to be done. Knowing that we are postponing the inevitable, we get depressed. When we are depressed, we feel alone. At such times, it is helpful to realize that the tendency to do routine work over important work is very common. Knowing that you are not hopelessly defective as a human being, but rather quite normal, can lead you to take the first steps towards getting started on your goals.

Realistic ambitions are easy to achieve

We have discovered one reason why we often find ourselves choosing to work on routine tasks, rather than important ones: We try to silence our conscience. But we may also choose routine work because we feel confident that we can get it done. Our Western culture demands that we lead useful lives. We are taught that work should provide us with the means to lead secure lives. We are not taught to expect that work should be enjoyable and stimulating, as well as useful. As a result our lives may not be as satisfying as they could be.

To obtain a more satisfying life we must learn to have realistic ambitions rather than idealistic ones. If you set your initial goals too high, the inertia you have to overcome to get started could paralyze you. It is better to review your important goals, and modify them so that they are obtainable. It may make more sense, for example, to thank a friend for a present by a telephone call, than wait for a moment that never comes to write a thank-you-card. By the same token, it is better to run your dirty car through a car wash, than to wait for an opportunity to wash and polish it by hand.

An unconventional answer

When an author of this book receives a letter requesting certain information, he writes his response directly on the letter that he has received. He then photocopies the letter, keeps one for his file, and returns the other one to the person who sent the letter. He handles the letter only once. The letter writer is impressed on receiving an immediate response to his inquiry. Instead of having to wait two or three weeks for a neatly typed letter, the letter writer will have the information requested in less time than he or she expected.

Be honest. What prevents you from reducing some of the pressures in your life by limiting some of your expectations about how well you should perform? Is everything that you do so important that it must be done perfectly? What would happen if the results of your efforts were not as fantastic as you expect them to be? It is important that the expectations you set for yourself be realistic, worth starting, satisfying to achieve, and satisfying for you while you are working to achieve them.

There is more than one way to reach a goal

A second major obstacle that prevents many people from getting started on an important project is an attitude that there is only one way that they can achieve the results that they want. If they combine this attitude with a concern that they do not know what the right way is, it becomes impossible for them to begin that project.

Just as "there are many ways to skin a cat", there are many ways to develop or market a product, cook a fish, furnish an office, paint a picture, or write a book. Whichever way you choose to begin an important project is probably about as good as any other. Don't wait for the perfect way of working to miraculously appear. Work as you think you should, without being too self-critical. It is more important that you start your project than how you start it.

The work sheet will fool you

We will now look at a simple but elegant tool that you can use to help you accomplish your tasks effectively. It is a work sheet. By its appearance, it is nothing more than a standard piece of paper. But by using this tool in a systematic way, you may begin to work in new directions. Among other things, you will be able to start your work more easily, arrange your ideas more systematically, focus your thoughts, and record what you have accomplished, in a way in which information is easily retrievable.

An example of a work sheet is illustrated over. Your work sheets should be designed to meet your own unique needs. They can include whatever artwork or graphic design you would like. The only rule to be followed is that they must always be available for your use. They will work for you as long as you can easily grab one, pick up a pencil, and get started on your work. Besides becoming a signal for you to begin your work, a work sheet will induce you to concentrate on what you are doing. As you write on the work sheet, your thoughts will become increasingly focused. Before you know it, you will be absorbed in your work. If it is convenient, you may construct a mind map on a work sheet. Regardless of how you begin your project, your thought processes will be moving in the right direction. In addition, having visible evidence in front of you that you have begun your project will give you a feeling of satisfaction.

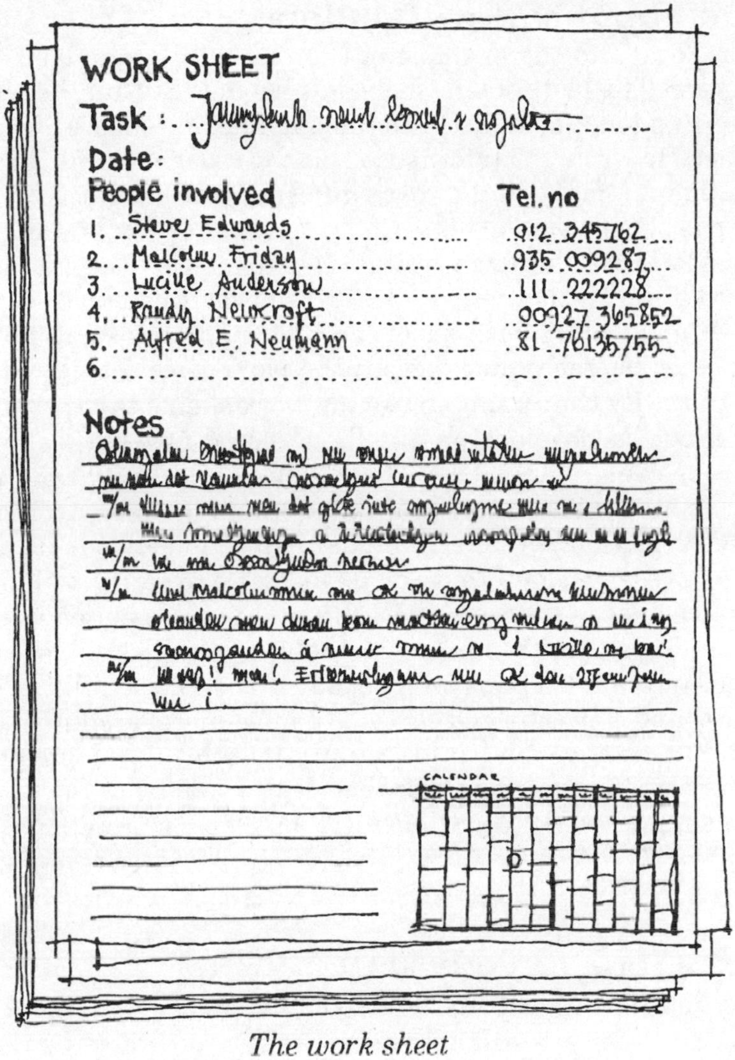

WORK SHEET

Task : *[handwritten]*

Date:

People involved   Tel. no

1. Steve Edwards 912 345162
2. Malcolm Friday 935 009287
3. Lucille Anderson 111 222228
4. Randy Neukroft 09927 365852
5. Alfred E. Neumann 81 76135755
6. ....

Notes

[handwritten notes, several lines]

[calendar illustration]

The work sheet

If while beginning this process you are somehow interrupted, your written notes will make it easier for you to return to your work. As you can see in our example, the work sheet has room for the names and telephone numbers of people you may have to contact to complete the task you have set out before you. Everything you add to it helps make the next step you take that much easier.

What about calling London

Let us return to the example of the marketing manager in the ship yard. The last time he looked at his Self Starter, he was inspired to phone for information about the Earls Court Show in London. He wrote the information on a work sheet, and used several others to make notes about different aspects of the trip. He used one sheet to make notes about transportation and hotel accommodation. Another sheet was used to identify the exhibits he wanted to see. Still another sheet was devoted to exploring London. After labeling each sheet, and jotting down some preliminary notes on each topic, he put the work sheets together, and filed them. By continuing to use his work sheets throughout the exhibition, he develops an excellent record of what happened, when the conference is over. He will have something tangible to draw upon to insure that he or others could have an even better and more productive time at similar exhibitions in the future.

We have discovered that you do not have to work in elaborate ways to achieve good results. So far, we have presented effective tools and systems that are pleasingly uncomplicated. We have learned new applications for a pencil and notebook, a WHAT-TO-DO list, and a pack of red cards. We have discovered how to expand our creative and intellectual skills by developing mind maps, Self Starters, and work sheets. It would be difficult to imagine simpler work tools that could give you more effective results.

Take a look at your watch

If you find that the advantages you gain from the tools we have discussed so far are still not enough to get you started on a particularly unpleasant task, here is what you can do. Take a look at your watch, and decide to work on that unpleasant job for just ten minutes. Then decide how you will reward yourself after the ten minutes of work. Take out your work sheet and... you are working! If you continue to work for more than ten minutes, you will certainly be forgiven. Do the same thing the next day, and so on, until the task is completed.

By applying this technique, you will feel less drained by guilt from having postponed your work. Exhaustion can result not only from doing too much, but from not doing the things that you should do, as well. Knowing that you have accomplished a lot during your work day will make you feel more alert and active after your day's work is done. If you feel that you were not able to accomplish much during your work day, you may find yourself coming home to collapse in your armchair, to escape into a magazine, television show, or whatever else may ease your feelings of exhaustion.

There is a risk that learning about techniques for getting started on your work may be too overwhelming for some people to handle. To reduce that risk, let's review what we have learned so far. First, we should rid ourselves of unrealistic expectations that tend to immobilize us. Second, we should recall the advantages of work sheets and other tools that can help us gain greater control over our lives. Third, we should recognize the advantages of thinking about difficult or unpleasant jobs in terms of manageable parts, instead of overwhelming entities. Finally, think positively. We will present many techniques and tools to help you manage your life.

The mechanical way

Today's managers recognize that man is not a machine. Yet, in some situations, it may be to our advantages to behave in a mechanical way. This is true when we wash, brush our teeth, dress, or greet acquaintances. It is also true when we engage in a number of activities at work. Earlier in this chapter we described the advantages of answering letters by automatically responding to them in a simple way. It may work you to your advantage to find other ways in which your work can be simplified by employing mechanical ways to respond to it.

Keeping things available

One of the greatest obstacles that can prevent us from getting started on a job comes from not having the information that is required to get the job done. We will look at this problem in the following chapters. It is our aim to give you better control of the information you need to get your job done by having better control of the way you gather and organize that information. The more organized you are, the more effectively you can get your work done. We expect that the techniques that we shall discuss may cause a minor revolution in your life.

Assisted by a glass of water

A consultant once advised a manager who had difficulty getting started on assignments to do the following:

* Place all of the material that you need to do the job on your desk.

* Sit down at your desk and pour a glass of water on your trousers.

* As you are now unable to stand up until the water has dried, you might as well work on your job.

10 Every paper in its proper place

You need the right information to make good decisions. A simplified decision making process is shown in the illustration over. It demonstrates the need to get information to the person who makes decisions. The quality of the decision is dependent upon the quality of the information that is obtained, as well as the skills of the decision maker, his or her ability to grasp and interpret what is going on in a situation, and the decision maker's interest in the matter at hand.

In this chapter, we will limit our discussion to examining methods that can help you obtain the information you need to make good decisions as quickly as possible. The importance of this activity should not be underestimated. The more difficult it is for you to obtain the information that you need to complete a job, the more reluctant you will be to get started on that job. In addition, the more appropriate the information is that you have, the greater the probability that decisions you make based on that information will be good ones. To achieve this we will explore another tool that will help you move in the direction that you would like to on the HOW-TO-DO-IT axis of the Model For Success.

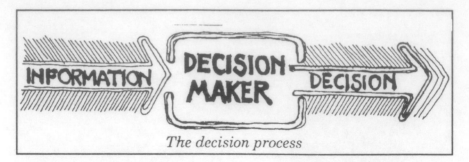

The decision process

Now you have to do some work

If you are willing to do the work presented, you will learn how to save time, and get more satisfaction from your job. The tool you will learn to use is similar to the ones we have discussed so far, spiced with an extra dose of common sense. It is easy to use, and gives instant results. The time these tools save you can be used for other things in your personal life, as well as in your work life.

The way to handle paper

There is a very simple principle for handling paper work. Until now, only a few people have really used it. If you begin to do so, we can assure you that you will find it to be a time saving device that will help you avoid many unpleasant situations. If you really do want to gain control over your work life, and free yourself from unnecessary distress, you should use the system for handling paper that we have illustrated above.

There are three things you can do with papers that you receive from your boss, co-workers, clients. other companies, government organizations, or any other source. You can save it, respond to it at once, or throw it away. If you receive a leasing contract for a company car, you can file it in a proper place so that you can retrieve it if you need it. If it is a pamphlet you receive for something you may need for your office, you can decide either to save the pamphlet where you hope you can find it if you need it, or throw it away. If you receive junk mail, you may be the kind of person who can find the courage and the wisdom to throw it away.

If you are not the sort of person who can throw junk mail away, you can gather up your courage by asking yourself "What

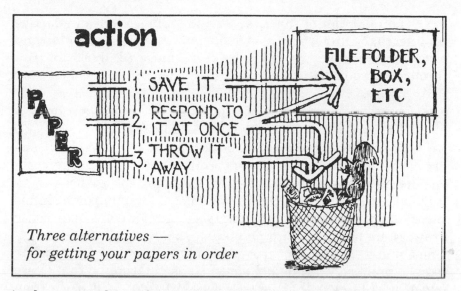

Three alternatives —
for getting your papers in order

is the worst thing that can happen to me if I throw this paper into the garbage?" If you decide that nothing terrible will happen to you, throw it away. When you have a smaller collection of papers to look through it will be easier to find the documents that you really need.

In our work lives and in our personal lives, we are faced with the recurring problem of when to throw paper away, and when to file it. This dilemma is not so simple to resolve. It is complicated by the fact that when we decide to save written material, we must be prepared to file it somewhere. This involves decisions about where to file papers, and what files and appropriate boxes to use. In reality, not many people have appropriate places set up to file the many kinds of written material they may choose to keep. Generally, people throw a lot of written material into the back of a drawer. Once it is there, most people do not have the courage to get rid of the papers they no longer need.

What alternatives do you have for collecting piles of papers in overstuffed drawers? Most likely, the solutions that you have come across were not effective. Perhaps you couldn't become motivated to apply yourself as you could, or the filing techniques were not very effective. For whatever reason, you found yourself stuck in the same mess as before. It is not surprising if you became discouraged and gave up trying to solve this problem.

In the reminder of this chapter you will discover an effective solution to the problem of how to file papers. You can develop and organize a system for filing papers that will work for you throughout your life.

What does he have in his drawers?

An author of this book has a desk with four drawers. In one drawer he has typewriter ribbons, rolls of calculator paper, carbon paper, and some other stationary supplies that are used regularly. In spite of the fact that he handles a lot of paperwork, his three remaining drawers are empty. You may wonder why these drawers are not filled with pamphlets, notebooks, letters, magazines, and other written paraphernalia. The reason is that he likes to practice what he preaches. He is determined that every paper or document that he saves must be put in a place from which it can be retrieved. He is, of course, often tempted to put all sorts of things in his empty drawers, promising himself to get to them later. At such times, he must remind himself about his determination to only save paper in its proper place.

It does not take long to learn how to use filing system we have developed. It takes an unacceptably long time to get work done if the filing system were to fall apart.

It only takes a few seconds

One tool that can help you save valuable time is a simple plastic, cardboard, or wooden box, such as you would use to store magazines.

Suppose you receive a pamphlet for some office supplies that you decide should be kept. If you have not already done so, take a box, and label it "Pamphlets For Office Supplies".This investment in your future will take no more than three minutes of your time. The next time you receive a similar pamphlet, you can put it in this box. It should take you no more than a few seconds. When you need the pamphlets, you can get them quickly. If these pamphlets do not have a place of their own, you probably would add them to the pile of papers in your drawers, closets, shelves, or garage. Even if you could remember that you have saved them when you need them, you probably would not be able to find them. You would waste time when looking for them, as well as when determining how to replace them. This tool can also prevent you from losing your temper, and becoming distressed and aggravated as a result of not being able to locate information when it is needed. If such small incidents can cause you aggravation, imagine the effects several incidents can have on you by the end of an average day.

You decide!

It is now time to decide which files and indexes you should identify and develop to meet your unique needs. Some files will be easy to identify. Most likely, you are not so certain about your need for many other files.

If you are managing a small company, you may appreciate a simple and effective method for handling invoices, banking and mailing records, salary information, vouchers, and other papers. Because such papers must be handled every day, it makes good sense to store them in files of their own. The system we shall introduce has the capacity to do this, as well as to store all other papers that you may come across in your daily routines.

It works for us

Over the years, we have examined many different kinds of filing systems. Not surprisingly, the most expensive or elaborate systems were not always the best ones. As our search for effective filing systems continued, it became apparent that filing systems containing similar kinds of material, such as invoices or order forms, are easy to develop. On the other hand, filing systems containing mixed materials are much more difficult to develop.

Before we began our search for an effective filing system, we generally relied on index files sectioned off with labeled plastic tabs. This system was unsatisfactory in many ways. For one, it is difficult to modify index files once they are in place. You may spend a few days developing such a system to get your papers into satisfactory order, only to discover a short time later that you have some papers to be filed that you have not developed a section for. The logical action is to make up another file title, put it on a folder, place the paper in it, file it in some fashion, and hope that you will be able to remember where you put it. But you know that you may not. Only a few days after developing it, your file index is outdated, and begins to collapse.

A filing system that works

Do not think that this topic is too unimportant to spend time on. On the contrary, gaining more control of important information and documents that you require is a very important topic for life management.

If you want to keep your papers in order, don't become too dependent on the filing system that we have just described. It is not flexible enough to handle the great variety of papers that must be filed over any period of time. Instead, learn how to use a system that is so flexible that you will be able to handle all papers that must be added to it. Any individual or organization can benefit from its use. A good filing system is of particular value to organizations that must stay abreast of our changing world. New products, marketing techniques, government regulations, and related data must constantly be incorporated into files, and retrieved when they are needed. The ability of your organization to keep up with these changes will be hindered or helped by the filing system that it uses.

We found one system that meets our criteria for being flexible and effective. It is particularly effective for filing many different kinds of papers. It is illustrated on page 102.

This entire filing system consists of large loose leaf binders. Each binder contains index files consisting of tabbed dividers, with a pocket attached to each divider. Each index file binder should contain approximately thirty pocketed dividers. Each index file binder may have a different general purpose. Three binders will contain 90 different sections for you to organize and file your papers in. When you first set up this system, it is doubtful that you will label all of the sections that you have room for.

The filing system that we are describing should be developed to meet your unique needs. Hard cover loose leaf ring binders come in many sizes, thickness, colors, and styles. A three to five inch binder can be purchases for just a few pounds. The file binder should be easy to use, but thick enough to store 30 sections with filled pockets. Dividers with tabs and pockets can be purchased in most office supply stores. The pockets should be strong enough to contain several papers that aren't able to be hole punched. Pocketed dividers should cost no more than a few pence each.

The front page of each index file binder should have a number of blank lines equal to the number of tabs within it. Each line should have a number written in pencil in front of it, corresponding to the 30 index pockets within the binder. A title and/or sentence describing what each file contains, should be written on the line corresponding to the order of the pocketed index tabs. You may choose to keep the content pages of several index file binders in the front of a single file binder.

Getting it together

Begin by developing an index file binder for a general area that you would like to keep tabs on. It can be related to work or to your personal life.

Whatever is put on the front index page of the file binder should be written in pencil, so that it may be easily erased. When you begin to construct your file binder, you may find that you at first need no more than ten pocketed index tabs for the binder. You can begin your filing system by filing a paper behind any tab, and recording the paper that is on the appropriate line of the index page. If possible, hole punch the material and secure it within the rings of the binder. If it cannot be hole punched, you may secure it by slipping it into the pocket of the file tab. Very similar material may be filed in the same section. Papers that are similar, but deserve to be in different files can be placed in index sections that are close to each other.

You will find it easier to develop your filing system if you spread the files you need throughout the binder. If for example, you begin by filing ten different papers, do so behind tabs 1, 5, 9, 13, 17, and so on, rather than behind tabs 1 through 10. In this way, as your file system develops you will be able to group similar sections together. Whatever you add to the system should be

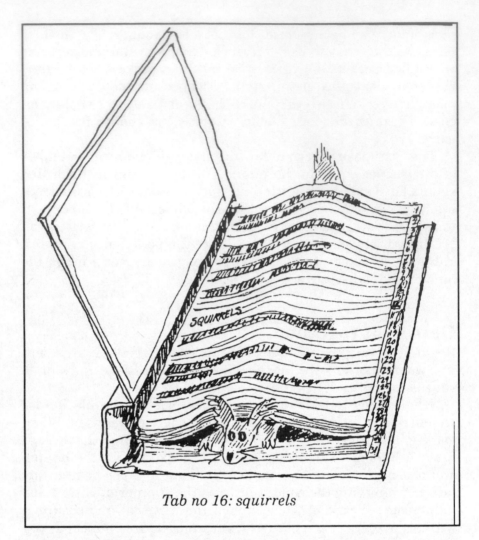

Tab no 16: squirrels

written in pencil in the appropriate place of the index page in the front of each file binder. When a paper no longer needs to be kept, take it out and erase what was written on the corresponding line of the index page.

As you can imagine, the differences between this system and the ones we have described before are vast. This system is very flexible. It allows you to keep track of many different kinds of papers that might otherwise be lost in the shuffle. It is easy to develop and use. The cover page records what and where important papers are kept. It is easy to review, modify and update anything within the system. The system can be easily expanded. It will not be outdated after it is first developed. File binders are easy to store and move around. The entire system is inexpensive to set up. It will serve you well for many years.

Now is the time

You will be surprised how this simple system can affect your life. Because you can easily retrieve information when you need it, you will be able to work more effectively, and experience less stress. Whatever parts of your life are in a mess can be straightened out once you have the right systems in place to do it. All of us can benefit from a system that allows us to retrieve important information when we need it, and to easily file documents and forms, without having to make aggravating decisions about how and where to do it.

Few people have their papers in order. Even if you have a system that you are fairly satisfied with, you can make a good system even better by adapting the techniques we have presented. If you are not satisfied with the way papers are handled in your life, this is the time to do something about it. If you don't do it now, you probably never will. Reserve a day to get started, get the materials you need, and do it.

One example

Let's explore how this system can be applied to the needs of a small company. If you were the owner of a distributing company, you could develop this system to meet your own unique needs.

Begin with no more than ten index files in a binder. Gather all of the loose papers you have scattered in your files, drawers, closets, and other hiding places. Identify the index headings that you need, and pencil them on the appropriate lines of your index cover. Start with the paper on top of your pile, and decide to throw it away or file it in an appropriate section of a file binder. If you miss a title when you first plan the sections headings, it is easy to modify the binder by using the space you have reserved for this purpose. After handling the first paper, file or discard the next one, and so on until all of your loose papers are gone. All unique records can be filed within the system that we have described. Copies of invoices, unpaid bills, mailing lists and other large groups of records may be placed in their own file binders. Journals, pamphlets, and related material can be placed in boxes, as described earlier.

Your life at present is affected by how you have prepared for it in the past. The effort you put into this system today, will pay off in the future. The time you spend on this and other tools described in this book will dramatically change the way you work.

It is necessary to expand upon this example. If you have a small company, it is worthwhile to adapt this system to meet your needs. In part, it is designed according to the way debt and credit entries are made. It can be used to keep account of information as diverse as salary records, vehicle expenses, and leasing contracts. It can also be used to catalogue every important paper that comes across your desk, no matter how unique it may be.

You will become an example to others

You now have a simple way to put all of your papers in a fixed place. What your index system will look like depends upon the types of documents you deal with. A sales manager, bank manager, teacher, doctor or lawyer will need an appropriate index to meet his or her unique professional needs.

Once you have discovered how valuable your index is, share your newfound tool with your associates. They may have suggestions how you can improve it. They may also be inspired to develop indexes of their own. Once your associates have completed their indexes, you both gain one more advantage: You are now able to understand and to share each other's filing system. This is a big advantage for you and your co-workers to have. The performance of your entire team will improve. You can help one another. Appropriate papers can be added to each other's files. It would not be surprising if a common filing system contributes to a better working relationship among your fellow workers as well.

The art of developing special projects

The system we have discussed works well for managing papers that you work with on regular basis. It is also useful as a tool for keeping track of special projects. Material for special projects are often mismanaged in the same way we mismanage other unique papers. They are placed in a desk drawer, on a shelf, or within some file where we hope to retrieve them when they are needed. If they do get misplaced, we hope that a copy can be retrieved by someone else.

Our file binder system has two advantages for dealing with special projects. First, we can use the system to store the projects. Secondly, we can use it to develop the projects.

A file binder can be very useful for developing special projects. The index sections can be used to contain reference material, drafts, notes and other data that must be kept in order and referred to when we were actively working on the project. Indexes can include the names and phone numbers of people involved in the project, time tables, letters, projected budgets, WHAT-TO-DO lists, and other related materials that we tend to search for every time we begin to act on the project. Every paper used in a project should have an appropriate place where it can be filed.

As your project develops, you will feel like an artist, creatively working from the palette of information that you have at your finger tips. As the left side of your brain becomes less anxious about losing track of the information that you need, the right side of your brain can begin to let your creative powers flow. You can let your imagination loose as to how the project should develop and the kinds of information and resources you choose to employ.

The index will also give form and stability to the project as it develops. Knowing that you have control over the way the project is developing will give you a secure feeling. The more secure you feel, the more you will be able to feel inspired. Once the project is completed, you have a record of everything you need, which can be used to your advantage when modifying the project, or when developing similar projects in the future.

A finished project can also be filed within an index binder like any other papers.

105

Where are we?

We have spent a good deal of time discussing how to sort papers. Once you experience the satisfaction of having the information that you need for work available when you need it, the time we devoted to this chapter will seem very worthwhile. This is an important tool for moving in the direction you want to go on the HOW-TO-DO-IT axis.

It is time to stop reading and to take action. Decide which day you will set aside to begin to get your files in order. It is now or never.

11 Your tools will also work at home

You have now brought some order to your office files. Your increased effectiveness at work should more than make up for the cost of the materials that your employer may have provided.

Why not organize your home files as well?

Consider the number and kinds of papers you have at home. If you have a need for handling information at work, you probably have an even greater need for handling information at home. Few people have an effective filing system for their personal and family papers. If you are like most people, you have piles of papers stacked in closets, drawers, trunks, boxes, and other strange places. You may have crammed several different files into the same drawer, or have important papers scattered among several unlabeled files.

We create many excuses for not having appropriate filing systems.

- We may not believe that it is important to keep files.

- Division of responsibility for keeping files may not be clear.

- We may think that it is impossible to have an effective filing system, and have given up making one.

- We don't know how to keep our files in order.

- We have been too stingy to get the materials that we need for an effective system.

- We don't want others to think of us as being too compulsive.

- Developing an effective filing system requires some effort, and it really doesn't have an urgent deadline, so we can always decide to put it off for another day.

Regardless of our reasons, we continue to suffer the consequences when we do not have an effective filing system. At the very least, it is irritating to be unable to find a warrantee for a camera, vacuum cleaner, or television when it breaks down. If we misplace a copy of our previous tax returns, a potential tax audit may be very disturbing. Misplacing an address or telephone number may be the beginning of the end of a relationship.

Hundreds of such problems will occur throughout our life if we do not give enough thought as to how to store our papers. It will result in unnecessary problems, add to our stress level, and waste our important spare time.

Gaining control over future time

Your floor is not a good place to store things

Before finding a system that works, our papers were in a terrible mess. One author stored his papers on the floor next to his tiny desk. When he moved into a new house, he decided that it was time to design a filing system that really worked. After exploring several alternatives, he successfully developed a system based on the principles discussed in the last chapter. He placed several bookshelves along the walls of his new study. He then developed several index binders, and placed all of the papers that he considered worth saving in them. He gathered boxes for magazines, pamphlets and similar materials. But in spite of his careful planning, the system did not turn out to be perfect. He found that there are many more kinds of papers that have to be filed at home than are filed in an average office. In many ways, the variety of papers needed to run a home is similar to the variety of papers needed to run a small company. More file categories had to be pencilled in from the beginning than he anticipated.

Once this correction was made, the author found that the system really worked. He felt less irritated when he had to locate important papers. He no longer lets papers pile up, but deals with them at once. It takes only a few moments for him to find the documents that he needs. He was even able to gather the information needed for his last income tax return in just a few minutes.

In the sections that follow, we will discuss what may be included among the categories of a home filing system.

Don't be stingy

Do not be stingy with yourself when you need materials and supplies for your home or your office. Get the papers, envelopes, stamps, binders, dividers and storage boxes that you need. The cost for most of your materials, will come to less than you would pay for a meal in a good restaurant. If you need a calculator or a typewriter, buy it! The longer you wait to get what you need, the less prepared you are to deal with the many situations that require them. Second hand equipment will do.

You also deserve to have a decent place to work on your home. It is virtually impossible to get work done if you do not have a place where you can work comfortably. Lighting should be adequate, so as not to cause you distress when you work. If you don't have the book shelves that you need, get some.

If you were the manager of a small company, you would know the importance of having a filing system to keep track of your papers. But when it comes to handling paper work at home, most people do not understand how important it is to keep track of important documents. Households may differ in many ways. Whether you live in an apartment, a house, a condominium, or a trailer, you will always have records to keep track of.

Our suggestions for keeping track of papers should of course be modified to meet your needs. If we omit an index title that you need, add it to your filing system. If we include a file that you do not need, eliminate it. We have listed sections titles that we use to arrange many of our most important papers. These papers are kept in three index binders. One binder is labeled "Personal Index File", another binder "Home Index File" and the third is labeled "Car Index File". You may find our suggestions to be a useful starting place for developing your own files.

Your Personal Index File

This index binder is designed to keep track of important documents and papers that have personal importance to you and your family. Label an index binder "Personal Index File". Add 50 tabbed dividers with pockets to the binder. You need at least two lined pages to serve as cover pages for this binder. Be sure to skip lines so that you may add appropriate sections at some later date. Wherever it is appropriate, pencil in the following section titles on the line of the cover page corresponding to its appropriate index file:

1. Personal and family information
2. Marriage and birth certificates
3. Health insurance documents and forms
4. Passports and passport photos
5. Membership cards
6. Health reports, certificates of vaccinations, etc...
7. Awards, certificates, and testimonials
8. Bank loans and interest forms (excluding mortgage loans)
9. Current monthly expense information
10. Retirement, social security, and pension planning information
11. Private loans, promissory notes, and interest agreements

12. Paid debts
13. Stocks, bonds, C.D.s, profit sharing plans, etc...
14. Credit card documents A
15. Credit card documents B
16. Credit card documents C
17. Credit card documents D
18. Unpaid bills, excluding mortgage
19. Paid bills, excluding mortgage
20. Subscription agreements
21. Private claims
22. Life insurance policies and premium forms
23. Health insurance policies and forms
24. Disability insurance policies and forms
25. Casualty Insurance policies and forms
26. Other insurance policies, excluding home owners
27. Information relating to income tax return for current year
29. Salary information
30. Holiday schedules and ideas
31. Legal documents (i.e., fines, tickets, court correspondence, etc.)
32. Professional organization correspondence
33. Birthdays, anniversaries, and other dates to remember
34. Ideas for presents for holidays and birthdays
35. Time tables for busses, trains, etc...
36. Lists of items to bring on vacations, trips, etc...
37. Certificates from schools, courses, programs, etc...

While reviewing our list, you may have thought of section titles for other papers that you would like to keep in this file. Take the opportunity to modify this list while your ideas are fresh in your head.

Your Home Index File

This index binder is designed to keep track of important documents and papers regarding your home, and the services and appliances that you need to run it.

Label an index binder "Home Index File". Add 50 tabbed dividers with pockets to the binder. As you did for your "Personal

Index File" prepare at least two lined pages to serve as cover pages. Remember to skip lines so that you may add appropriate sections at some later date. Pencil the following section titles on the line of the cover page corresponding to its appropriate index file:

1. Purchase contract
2. Inspection reports
3. Correspondence out
4. Correspondence in
5. Proof of purchase
6. Warrantee and Guarantees
7. Instructions for handling household appliances
8. Plans
9. Home owners insurance
10. Other insurance for the home and its contents
11. Heating bills
12. Electric bills
13. Water bills
14. Lawn and garden maintenance bills
15. Telephone bills
16. Pest control bills
17. Other bills for home maintenance
18. Mortgage loans
19. Bank loans
20. Assessment certificates
21. Survey information
22. Home improvement ideas
23. Repair history (e.g. amount and colors of paint needed)
24. Energy tips
25. Names and addresses of repairmen and service groups
26. Home owners association
27. List of valuables
28. Photos of valuables

Take time to review this list, and modify it in any way that helps you to keep the records that you need.

Your Car Index File

This binder is designed to keep track of important documents and papers regarding your automobiles.

Label an index binder "Car Index File". Add 30 tabbed dividers with pockets to the binder. Prepare a cover page, and pencil the following section titles on the line of the cover page corresponding to its appropriate index file:

1. Titles and proof of ownership
2. Repair booklets and instructions
3. Insurance
4. License and inspection information
5. Guarantees, warrantees and certificates
6. Gasoline bills
7. Repair bills
8. Rust protection
9. Tax information
10. Repair history
11. Road maps
12. Toll receipts
13. Parking receipts
14. Names and telephone numbers of service organizations and repair shops
15. Automobile club information

Again, this list of section titles should be modified to meet your own needs.

Clean your drawers and closets

Give yourself a weekend to get all of your filing done. The index descriptions that we have given you should make it easy for you to develop your initial file systems.

After you have set up your file binders and labeled your cover pages and index tabs, gather all of the papers that you have scattered in your closets, drawers, old files, corners, pockets, and wallet. Put them in a pile, and starting with the paper on top, place each piece in your new system or throw it away.

By the time you are finished, you will feel marvelous. You will have gained control over a part of your life that could have caused you some real problems. You will have also put yourself into a better financial position. It will be easier for you to keep track of tax deductible receipts. You can compare insurance costs from competing companies. Bills can easily be reviewed for accuracy. Proof for insurance claims is readily available. Repair costs can be reduced by using warrantees and guarantees you otherwise could not locate. Above all, you have attacked many of the sources of daily stress which have plagued you for years. The effects these stressors have had on your physical well-being must also be considered. They may even effect your health and life span.

Gaining control of your records will also give you more spare time. If your new system saves you three hours of searching for papers or struggling to correct problems that have emerged as a result of missing information each week, that adds up to 150 more hours to be used as you like each year.

Enjoy your new found time in the best of spirits and in the best of health.

Part D

Take a look around you

Take a look around you

We have examined the two dimensions of our Model For Success. We have seen how we can tap into thought processes that we rarely take advantage of, and apply simply but effective tools to help us identify WHAT-TO-DO to reach our goals. We have learned how to motivate ourselves to get on course for our goals, and to stay on course with easy to use techniques such as the Self Starter. Once we can identify WHAT-TO-DO, and feel motivated to do it, we can determine HOW-TO-DO-IT. We familiarized ourselves with methods to help us achieve good results, such as work sheets and effective information retrieval and filing systems.

Congratulations!

Your ability to accomplish work in a rapid and effective way is now enormous. It is more than likely that people around you have begun to notice that you are gaining control of your life.

You are doing fine!

We could stop our program here. Most likely, you are more relaxed, and more effective in your daily routines than you were before you opened this book. But there are some important life management issues that we have not yet explored. One issue focuses on your environment. We shall examine how your work environment affects you, and what you can do to control it. We shall begin our discussion by taking a look at your desk.

12 Clear your desk

The tools we have presented in previous chapters were designed to help you organize your thoughts. We will now turn our attention to some tools and techniques to help you organize your environment. We will begin by looking at some simple techniques to get your desk into order.

Take a good look at your desk. Why does it look the way it does? What is on top of it, and why is it there? Do you have a system for placing things on your desk, or do you improvise? Can you remember why you bought those plastic organizers that look so awkward? Why do piles of paper grow on it so often?

People often put paper on and around their desks in order to remind themselves to take care of different things. In the beginning, this system may even work. But after a while, the amount of work in each pile becomes so great that we can no longer keep track of what is in them. We may have to search through piles of papers several times to locate a specific page. When we finally find it, we may discover that it is out of date, or overdue.

We do not have to continue to work in this way. It is very difficult to work on one project, and at the same time be reminded of all the other things that have to be done. It is distressing and demotivating to arrive at work and spend the day staring at a symbol of disorganization.

A lifetime of searching

Some people take pride in their disorderly desks. They claim that they know exactly where each paper is kept. They are absolutely right. All of their papers are on their desks! The problem is that it takes minutes to locate whatever they need. How many minutes do they lose searching for what they need every day? How much of their time is wasted each week, month, year, or during their lifetime?

Of course the mess on your desk will not stop you from working. There are margins for error in almost every job, and you are allowed to spend some time on unnecessary work. There are plenty of efficient people who work at desks piled up with papers. But they can be even more efficient if they alter their way of working, and use the method we shall describe. If they do so, they need never be depressed by the sight of their own messy desk again.

What is your system?

In a previous chapter, we asked you to think about how you store your papers. We would now like you to think about how you deal with work that comes across your desk.

Some people think that working at a desk that can't be seen is a status symbol. There are better ways of gaining status in your office. These ways are in direct conflict with the results that you get from a messy desk. If you are determined to keep piles of paper on your desk, you can still benefit from the simple method for organization that we will now describe. It has been used by hundreds of people who have attended our programs. The results they have reported are more than satisfactory. Still, there are some words of warning we will save for the end of this chapter.

Clear everything off of your desk, except for the papers you need for the work in progress. Get six containers large enough to hold your papers. You can use plastic, cardboard, metal, or wooden boxes that conceal their contents and can be easily stored. Try to avoid open letter boxes that are stacked on one another. You may put the boxes on your desk, in its drawers or on a shelf beside it.

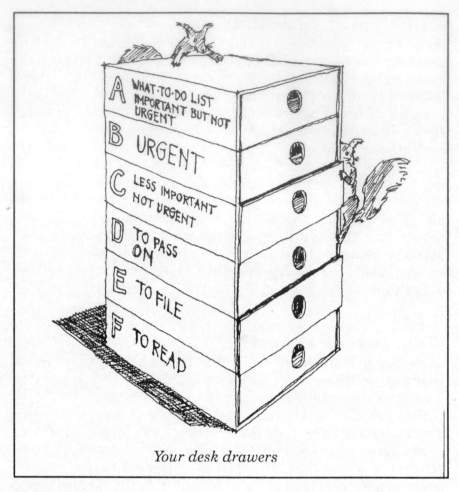

Your desk drawers

Your six boxes
Label the boxes:

A. **Important but not urgent; WHAT-TO-DO list**
B. **Urgent**
C. **Less important, not urgent**
D. **To pass on**
E. **To file**
F. **To read**

A. Important but not urgent

This is your most important box. All of the important papers you will work with in the near future are placed in this box. These papers are related to work that is often pushed aside for urgent, but less important matters. The more you deal with the important papers in this box, the more successful you will be. This box will also contain your WHAT-TO-DO list. The fact that you keep this list along with your most urgent papers will remind you how important the information on the WHAT-TO-DO list is, and that it must be done without delay.

You can become more successful by beginning every working day by selecting an important job from this box. You will feel energized for the rest of the day, knowing that you have accomplished something that is really important. You did not postpone what had to be done. You began your day free of slavery to urgent but unimportant tasks.

Important tasks often require planning. One hour of planning may save you many hours of extra work. It is difficult to think of a more profitable way of using your time than for planning. But planning alone is not enough! Good managers must also consider how to organize their work and the work of others, how to review and to simplify it, how to promote good working relationships among staff members, and a hundred other matters that may be important, but are not always urgent. Many of these important tasks are never done because the manager does not know how to begin them.

Our system gives the manager a way to take care of these important matters. They may be written on the WHAT-TO-DO list, or be added to the Urgent priority box. Once they are there, you can begin to work on them with the tools that you have learned to use in this book.

B. Urgent

Any papers that must be dealt with in the near future should be placed in box B. They are usually simple to take care of, and require little effort. After starting your day by working on a task from box A, complete something from this box next. You may choose to work on assignments from this box when you would like a change of pace from whatever else you may be doing.

C. Less important, not urgent

Put whatever is somewhat important, bu not urgent into this box. Once each week, go through this box to see what has to be done. If you find that something has become urgent, handle it at once, or move it to box B. If material is no longer relevant, discard it.

D. To pass on

Place whatever papers are to be passed on to other people in this box. At the end of the day, pass all papers that did not have to be passed on sooner to whoever they go to. Using this system saves a surprising amount of time otherwise wasted by running off to someone else's desk when there is no need to.

E. To file

Papers that are to be placed into files or other indexes should be placed in this box. Anything in this box is there because you have chosen to put it in a permanent place. If you do not have a permanent place for a paper in this box, it is easy to develop one by using the system we discussed in the previous chapter.

F. To read

Place any papers that you have to read in this box. Whenever you need a rest, or just feel like reading, take the papers out this box and go through it.

A new experience - a clean desk

We have identified the six boxes that can change your desk. The boxes can be kept in any suitable place that is near you. They are not expensive.

Anything that you keep in the piles of your desk can be placed either in a file box, in your filing system, or in the waste paper basket. Every loose paper will be removed from your desk, to be placed where it belongs. No paper will be put on your desk unless it is necessary to have it at that moment. You will enjoy the advantages of a clean desk, and find that the system is easy to maintain. Ongoing jobs which are not yet finished can be placed into envelopes, and put in box A or box B. The system can be stretched to suit your needs. As long as it helps you to keep your desk clean, it is effective.

Too simple to discuss?

It is strange that managers give so little attention to paper management. Perhaps they are embarrassed to talk about such a simple topic. Never-the-less the most beneficial management programs often deal with paper management.

Think about the desks that are in the offices of organizations around the world. Each of the millions of desks is ruled by a different system - or ruled by the lack of any system. It is not satisfying or constructive for any human being to face a desk in the morning that is covered with papers. It can be stimulating to begin your work at a clean and organized desk. Imagine what a difference it would make if clean desks became the rule rather than the exception. Until this occurs, it is not surprising that so many people see work as a dirty word.

The six box system that we have described can also be used in organizing papers in your home. It can be great help for family record keeping. It can also be used to teach your children how to keep their papers in order. Share this system with them except for boxes C and D.

A word of warning

No system is perfect. Our experience has taught us that this system has some pitfalls that you should be aware of.

The boxes must only be used as a temporary place for papers to be kept. Papers should not be kept in them for long periods of time. There are a number of things that you can do to avoid this from happening. First, be sure to follow the principles that determine where papers are to be placed. If your papers are in the right box, your chances of losing track of them are greatly reduced. Second, if you use the index system that we have described, you need not get stuck wondering where a paper should be filed. As the index file binders are designed to expand recording to your needs, you will be able remove papers from your boxes with very little difficulty. Third, review what is in each of your top boxes daily. If you do, you will continue to put important papers in the box A and urgent papers in box B. If you don't, you will not dare to put papers which you intend to work with in the near future in these boxes. Instead, you will begin to build up piles of papers again. Discipline yourself so that you do not transform these boxes into another storage system. All that you have to do is check the contents of the boxes marked "important" and "urgent" on a regular basis.

13 Think without being disturbed

Let's continue to discuss the environment. It is not always enough to know WHAT-TO-DO and HOW-TO-DO-IT. We cannot succeed in achieving our goals if our environment is not satisfactory.

You now have a clean desk at which to work and the tools to work with. It is now time to get the peace and quiet that you need to work effectively. This is one of the rarest commodities in an office today. Many people have thought a lot about this problem, while others decided that it is too difficult to try to solve.

Let us begin our discussion with the following common assumptions:

- It is desirable to work without being disturbed.
- It is important to have a friendly atmosphere in the office.
- Your telephone should be used in an effective way.
- Telephone calls may often interfere with your work.
- A manager must be available when needed.
- A manager must be allowed time for planning.

Although all of the above statements are true, they are often contradictory. A manager needs time for planning, but at the same time must be available whenever he or she is needed. Studies have shown that on an average, managers work undisturbed for no more than eight minutes at a time. It is difficult to deal with important matters within such short time periods. Even worse, many managers will not even begin to work on important matters until they feel that they have enough time to devote to them. When that time never comes, a crisis may occur. Stress, guilt, and disagreements that accompany crisis often go home with people after work.

Problems that result from contradictory assumptions about work can only be solved through compromise. We must each determine for ourselves how to meet our own needs, as well as the needs of other people. In most cases, it is advisable for a manager to reserve an hour or two for their own work every day. It may be possible to do this between 9.30 - 10.30 in the morning, and between 1.30 - 2.30 in the afternoon. During these hours, a manager should attempt to work undisturbed with the tasks at hand. If it can be arranged, a receptionist or a secretary should take incoming calls at such times. He or she should note who phoned, what it was about, whether and when the call can be returned, and inform the caller when the manager can be reached. Important calls should of course be received immediately. As time goes on, most of the manager's calls will come in at the fixed times when the manager is available for them.

Just thinking!

We will rarely disturb someone who is working hard. We will not interrupt an engineer while he is welding, a chef preparing food in a fine restaurant, a teacher in the middle of a lesson, or a surgeon during an operation, without sufficient reason and an apology. Yet people have few reservations about disturbing a manager while performing his or her most important function. That function is thinking.

Is a marketing manager puzzling over marketing plans for next year, or a principal trying to sort out a spring syllabus allowed to work undisturbed? Probably not. As long as they are at their desks, they are fair game. Although most managers may think that it is wrong to take stamps from work for their personal use, they do not give a second thought about stealing time from an associate involved in problem solving.

It is time for a change in attitude regarding time periods managers need for thought. Disturbing people who are working with unnecessary visits robs co-workers, the organization, and yourself of the most valuable commodity in any company - time to think!

"And then Pat said..."

The importance of the angle of the door

Many organizations have an open door policy to demonstrate that they are conscientious towards meeting the needs of their employees. As ridiculous as it may seem, we have all met people who think that this policy has to do with the angle that a door is kept open. They believe that a manager who keeps his or her office door open at a 45 degree angle is a better manager than one who keeps the office door open at a 10 degree angle.

You do not have to cater to such silly assumptions. If you are a manager who works more effectively with a closed door, close it! If you feel that you gain more control over your work by occasionally closing your door, it is to the advantage of your associates, the organization, and yourself that you do it. As a manager,

127

it is your duty to use the resources at your disposal to achieve the goals of the organization. One of your resources is a door. If you are concerned about closing it when you need adequate time for thought, it may be time to start questioning how effective you are as a manager.

You will congratulate yourself

If you need undisturbed time for work, but do not have it, the first thing you can do is to speak with your supervisor to get his or her support. Most supervisors will appreciate an employee who wishes to modify a working style in order to achieve better results. Together, you may work out a plan that will allow you to have longer periods of time for undisturbed thought. If your office does not have a door, you may agree for instance, that a "Do Not Disturb" sign is an adequate device for you to use. While you are meeting, you may also be encouraged to make other suggestions that may benefit the organization.

Once you succeed in obtaining undisturbed time for planning and problem-solving, you will congratulate yourself. When you first begin to use the time you have for thoughtful work, you may be disturbed with it. As you think about starting an important task, you may even wish that someone would interrupt you. If this happens use your Self Starter and other motivation tools to begin your work. Within a few days, you will wonder why you waited so long to get a clean desk, the tools you need to work, and the time to do it in.

Once again we must add a word of caution. The desire to have time-on-your-own should not be pushed to extremes. If someone wishes to reach you on an important matter, it must be possible to do so. In most cases, one or two hours a day is sufficient for undisturbed time to get important matters taken care of.

I think I need the telephone

We have all met managers who never have time for managerial work. We sometimes wonder if they prefer it that way. Their telephones are often used as an excuse to postpone working on important jobs. They appreciate receiving phone calls when they have no reason to call anyone themselves. If the phone does not ring, a visit to a co-worker may serve as a suitable excuse to ignore work.

Why do some managers do almost anything to avoid having undisturbed time to work on important tasks? While managers find it difficult to begin working on important tasks, others want to be perceived as being busy and indispensable. By working under pressure, they fool themselves into thinking that they are important. They prefer to be seen by associates as working all of the time. Telephone calls, visitors, and interruptions are welcome. When they get a quiet moment to work, they feel anxious and confused about what to do.

The attitude that we are describing may be the result of a common but misguided approach to work. When we judge our performance and that of our co-workers, we must ask if we are more concerned with the activities that are being carried out, or the results that are being achieved.

Two extremes

Some managers always want to be at the disposal of other people. They believe that it is important to be able to help people at all times. In reality this attitude may make the manager less able to help people in the long run. A candle that burns at both ends burns out quickly. A manager who becomes involved in everything may be reluctant to delegate when it is called for. We have seen managers use qualified secretaries only for basic clerical purposes. They do not give them appropriate assignments to reduce their own work loads.

Other managers go to the opposite extreme. One manager would never answer a phone call unless his secretary was unable to satisfy the caller's needs. He gave his secretary full reign on how to respond to the caller. The risk that this manager took is that important information that can only be obtained by informal means may have never reached him. Too many filters between a manager and the environment will prevent information that is necessary for good decision making to get through.

Managers must determine for themselves how involved they should be in their work environment. Too much exposure may keep the manager too busy with mundane matters to be effective. Too little exposure may result in inappropriate decision making. The best way to protect yourself from either of these traps is to be aware that they are there.

The strength to say no

As we have discussed, the need to work without being disturbed is not the same as a desire to work without other people. We have discussed the value of having periods of time during your work day to work on important matters without being disturbed. We have also discussed the importance of staying in touch with your working environment so that you are aware of relevant changes within it.

It is not easy to tell people that you are busy. You may be afraid of offending them. But ask yourself how you would react if you visited a co-worker and he politely asked to see you after he has finished his task. We doubt that you would feel angry or hurt in such a situation. You might even respect the ability of the co-worker to say so, and wish that you had the strength to do the same in similar situations.

If a stubborn colleague continues to disturb you with unnecessary visits, do not hesitate to say that you are busy at the moment, and work out a mutually agreeable time to meet. Telling the person this at once will give you control over your time, and will prevent you from becoming irritated.

The early bird catches the worm

If you have trouble beginning important work during the day, you may consider working beyond normal working hours occasionally. One way to work without being disturbed is to arrive at the office before the start of the normal working day. If anyone else is there, they have probably come in early to work as well. This is not always the case with people who stay at work after others have left. As some people stay after work to meet friends they have arranged to go out with, they may take the opportunity to chat with you while killing time. But if you choose to spend a few evenings during the week for planning, you will still be satisfied with the results. A productive evening of important work can turn stressful concerns into satisfaction with results.

Maybe on a Sunday

If you would like to change a routine that you are dissatisfied with, you may consider going to the office on a Saturday or Sunday or on a holiday. If you use that time for some effective planning, you may be paid back with even more spare time in the future.

People come up with clever ideas for finding time for undisturbed work. We know one manager who takes a later lunch hour than his co-workers. He has not only found an hour during which he can work undisturbed, but he can also enjoy his lunch in quieter and less stressful conditions than usual. Other managers make the time they need for undisturbed work by shortening time spent on time wasting activities, such as unnecessary phone conversations. It is embarrassing to forget why you phoned, after talking with another party for half an hour. One way to avoid such situations is to prepare for calls that you must make by listing on a piece of paper what you would like to talk about. For best results, check off each point as it is made.

The mail is a resource

It is not always easy to reach people by telephone. Sitting near a phone is not the only activity business people are engaged in. Some people become obsessed with reaching others by telephone. They will use sophisticated redialling devices, and continue to try to reach someone for days until they succeed. They do not care how many hours are spent in the process, what the cost is, or how irritated they become until they reach their designated party. It does not occur to them that there is another way to achieve their goals. It is called the mail.

Letters and memos have a number of advantages over the telephone. You can communicate with another party through a single action rather than through a number of attempts. Your message will be clear and concise. You do not have to disturb a person who may be involved in important thought. There is a

131

useful record of what is communicated. Written messages tend to be taken more seriously than verbal ones. They are inexpensive to use. They can be written whenever you feel inspired. You can use personalized stationery to communicate your style and image.

We are not, of course, recommending that you substitute letters and memos for telephone calls in all situations. But becoming aware of the advantages of letters and memos, you have an alternative to the often useless activity of chasing people around on the telephone.

Eight hours are enough

Some people cannot work without being disturbed during regular office hours. We know of an accountant who believes that the worst place to work is in his office. He prefers to work at home two days every week. Only his secretary knows how to reach him there.

We have already discussed people who prefer to work outside regular working hours. If such work periods become habitual, something may be wrong. Eight hours a day should be more than enough time to get through your work. The more you follow the advice within this book, the less extra hours you should need to complete your work. If this does not occur, it may mean that you prefer your work life over your personal life, which is an entirely different problem than this book is concerned with.

It's time to relax

We have already discussed some of the harmful effects of stress. Programs that teach managers how to deal with stress generally emphasize two ways to achieve results. One way is to gain better control of the work environment. the other way is to learn how to relax. Most of this book has been devoted to giving you the tools that you need to gain greater control over your work environment. In the next chapter, we will present methods to help you relax.

The best way to gain control over your life is to practice the methods that we have presented in this book. You have all the techniques you need to choose WHAT-TO-DO, HOW-TO-DO-IT, obtain and maintain the information that you need, begin your work, and find the time in which to do it.

It is time to relax, and to recover from the harmful effects stress has had in the past.

Part E

How to reduce stress

14 What is stress?

We hope that you are successfully using the Model For Success to do the right things in the right ways. We also hope that you have created a better working environment for yourself, and manage to control periods of time to work without being disturbed. The more you meet these goals, the greater your chances are for success in your personal and work life.

But if you are still not moving towards the level of success that you wish to achieve, it is time to examine how stress may be hindering your success, and what can be done to pull yourself out of the rut that you are in. The first step for climbing out of a rut is to understand the nature of what you are stuck in. We shall begin by examining what stress is, what causes stress, and what can be done to reduce it. By learning methods to reduce stress, you will be able to regain your piece of mind. The greater your piece of mind, the more prepared you will be to handle situations which cause stress. You will also be better prepared to use the tool that you now have to gain greater control over your life, which in turn will continue to decrease the stress that effects you.

Stress is natural
Stress is a natural part of our lives. It is our bodies' reaction to the stimulation we are receiving from the world around us. We all need a certain amount of stimulating in order to become mo-

tivated to get things done, and to feel satisfied with ourselves. As Freud wrote, we don't take on difficult tasks unless we are motivated to do so. Each of us requires a different amount of stimulation to function best and be happiest. When we receive too much stimulation, we become bored. If we become too bored for too long, we feel depressed. When we receive too much stimulation, we become anxious, or depressed. If we become too anxious or depressed, we become distressed.

Both the quantity and the quality of the stimulation that we receive can affect us. The single circumstance of losing a job will obviously be more stressful than having to write 20 letters in a single evening. Stimulation that puts us under great strain or stress is called a stressor. Internal stressors come from within ourselves. They are often the result of difficult demands and expectations we create for ourselves. External stressors come from the sources outside of ourselves. They may come from demands made by our families, friends, supervisors, co-workers, and clients. When causes of stress do not go away, acute stress will give us a stereotypic reaction. This means that we will continue to react as if we are under great stress, no matter how little stimulation we may be under. We may overreact to minor situations around us, resulting in greater problems, increased stress, and an unpleasant life.

You have two nervous systems

If it were not for stress, humans would have disappeared long ago. When our ancestors were in danger, the adrenaline secreted into their blood by their adrenal glands prepared them for a fight or for flight. Once the threat was dealt with, their bodies returned to normal.

Stress reactions are carried through the autonomic nervous system. The autonomic nervous system consists of two parts: the sympathetic nervous system, and the parasympathetic nervous system. The sympathetic nervous system increases the body's reactions during a stressful situation. Stress reactions through this system may lead to muscular spasms, headaches, cramps, and back aches. The exact nature of the physical symptoms that an individual may experience as a result of stress will depend on

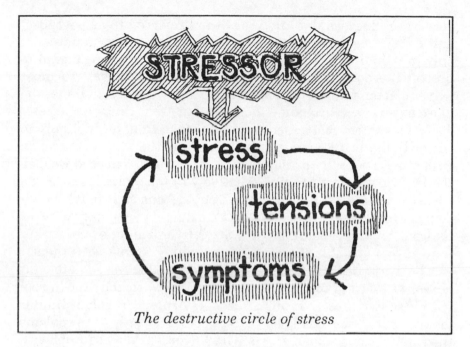

The destructive circle of stress

many factors, including the person's history and physical condition. Although stress is universal, the way it affects us is unique for every individual.

The parasympathetic nervous system helps return the body to normal after it has reacted to a stressful situation. It restores balance, and works to calm us down. If the parasympathetic nervous system is not able to eliminate stress symptoms, we will continue to experience stress long after the stressor that caused it is no longer around. The more we know how to activate this system, and how to deactivate the sympathetic system, the better we can control the effects of stress on our body, work, and life.

Stress symptoms are warning signals

Many people will visit a doctor with symptoms that cannot be explained by physical causes. Such symptoms are often stress related. A healthy individual will suffer from bodily stress symptoms when exposed to situations that are very difficult or impossible to handle. As a result of such situations, the body can become physically affected by various kinds of stress related problems. When the body and the mind begin to affect each other, the illnesses that may result are referred to as psychosomatic. Psychosomatic illnesses are very real. They do not exist only in the mind. Stress symptoms serve as a warning signal to protect the body from serious or additional damage. We must learn to listen to these signals. The sooner we listen to them, the more able we are to change the conditions that cause us stress.

When we feel distressed, we must learn to listen not only to our body, but to other people as well. One of the best ways to deal with stress is to talk to other people. The more distressed we feel, the less we are able to think creatively to solve problems. When we are bothered by a problem, we tend to focus on it to the exclusion of everything else around us. Our tunnel vision may prevent us from finding a solution that a relative, friend, or co-worker may have no trouble seeing if we are willing to talk with them.

The worst thing we can do when we feel distressed is to shut ourselves off from the rest of the world. Then, we may try to deal with its symptoms through alcohol, drugs, or some similar means. Such methods keep us from dealing with the problems that are the cause of our stress. The longer we delay dealing with the real causes of stress, the greater our problems become. The sooner we decide to solve our real problems, the sooner stress symptoms will disappear. Only then can we free ourselves from an unhappy life style.

Frustrations are distressing

Research demonstrates that involvement in social situations can be very stressful. The better we can handle ourselves in such situations, the less stress we experience as a result of them. Friendships begin with expectations of how other people behave. If these expectations are not fulfilled, problems may result. The unexpected behavior of such people confuses us, and causes us to question our own ability to judge others.

Distress resulting from unfulfilled expectations has even greater implications when we consider the many demands that we make on others, the demands we make on ourselves, and the demands others make on us. When these demands are not met, we feel the effects of stress. We also become distressed when we are not sure WHAT-TO-DO or HOW-TO-DO-IT what is needed

138

to meet these demands. Unfulfilled demands are stressful whether they come from outside or from within ourselves.

Stress is also related to the extent we are able to make decisions for ourselves. The less we are able to determine what jobs we should do and how they should be done, the greater our risks of suffering from stress. We feel distressed if we are not able to determine the extent of our own work load.

Stress researchers have found that the amount of harm caused by stress in the environment will vary from one individual to the next. The extent that an individual is hurt by stress will depend on many factors. These factors include the support the individual gets from other people, and the ease with which problems can be discussed. Because entrepreneurs often walk alone, with few people around to ease their fall when they have one, they are subject to high levels of stress. They can protect themselves to some degree by learning to confide in people around them. No matter how independent we may pride ourselves to be, there are times when we must depend on others. The support of others is important for everyone.

The perceptive manager

A manager who is responsible for the well-being of others can do many things to reduce the effects of stress on employees and improve the quality of their work. Allowing mature employees increased responsibility to make decisions for themselves, and then giving them the support they need to make things happen will reduce their stress and improve their work. You can also achieve these results by having groups of mature employees practice the exercises in chapter 21. Encourage them to be open towards each other, and free to express themselves constructively. They should know that employees who are not able to express their need for support will never get the support they need.

Our prehistoric ancestors had it easy

Stress signals alarm us from danger. In prehistoric times, our ancestors were aroused by stress signals to cope with danger. Stress signals disappeared once danger was gone. For modern man the situation is quiet different. Today's managers cannot eliminate the causes of stress the way prehistoric hunters could. If an employee believes that a supervisor or colleague is an enemy, he cannot destroy the enemy with a simple blow to the head. He cannot rely on his parasympathetic nervous system to bring his stress level back to normal, as his enemy lies dead at his feet. Instead, the employee continues to live with his or her disagreeable colleague, supervisor, family member, or neighbor until stress becomes a common state of affairs, rather than an exception to be dealt with. The body continues to suffer and to become exhausted. The greater the exhaustion, the less the body's immunity defenses can protect it from disease. It becomes more susceptible to infections, viruses, and diseases.

Death by stress

In the beginning of this century death from diseases such as pneumonia, tuberculosis, and influenza were very common. Today people rarely die from these diseases. Instead people die from other diseases which tend to be stress related. These diseases include asthma, ulcers, heart attacks, and cancer. Medical researchers are becoming increasingly interested in the relationship between stress and disease. Some researchers have even suggested that 80 percent of all diseases are caused by stress.

Stress thrives in our Western culture. We admire people who are successful. We are taught that success can be measured by the amount of money a person makes. Many people subject themselves to incredible stress in their attempts to become successful. They choose a life style in which they may be literally killing themselves to attain what they have been told they should want. But there is a way out of this pathetic situation. The more we know about stress, what causes it, and how it can be reduced, the better we can learn to manage it.

Effective planning reduces stress

Nobody really knows the total cost of stress to our society today. Obviously, the cost must be enormous. Time lost because of illness, production errors, poor communication, and accidents represents only the tip of the iceberg. In the United States, it is estimated that loss of production resulting from stress and stress related diseases may be as high as 50 billion dollars each year.

Such losses can be reduced. The more we understand how stress effects us, and how it effects organizations, the better prepared we will be to deal with it. Employees and managers who effectively plan their work, communicate clearly, and promote good relationships with their co-workers will reduce the stress within their own organizations. People who gain better control over their work lives by following the advice in this book will find their stress symptoms decreasing, and eventually disappearing. Combating stress by working on problems that cause it, with the resources that you need to get the job done, can be very effective.

Anxiety can change your life

As we have stated, it is not always harmful to be exposed to stress. Stress motivates us to solve our problems. Stress also motivates us to succeed at work, develop and nurture relationships, write books, and raise families. It forces us to turn off the television to paint the house. Constructive levels of stress do not harm our bodies. They help us to grow.

At high levels, stress can be destructive, making us very anxious or ill. At low levels, anxieties can be productive. They can shake us up, and force us to change our way of living. Even when we have trouble recognizing our own anxieties, others can recognize them. By communicating with other people we can learn much about ourselves.

Help yourself

What can be done to help people who suffer from stress?

Many people suffering from stress related symptoms seek the help of doctors. To some extent, a physician may help to relieve stress. But it is not possible for the average doctor to get a clear picture of the life style of his or her patient. Without that picture, it is difficult to make suggestions for necessary changes.

Work related stress can be reduced through the sources it comes from. If the level of stress is too high throughout the organization, key managers within the organization must accept responsibility for relieving it. They will take this responsibility once they understand the cost of stress to the organization and to its employees. But key managers cannot eliminate organization-wide stress problems by themselves. The cooperation of employees throughout the organization is required to reduce it. Work stress is eliminated when each employee begins to solve his or her own work related problems, and then moves on to solving problems involving relationships with others. Before we can claim responsibility for correcting the work habits of anyone else, we must first take the responsibility of correcting our own. If we don't, we will become cynical, and unable to improve our work life.

So far, this book has given you many tools to solve work related problems by gaining control over your own personal work environment. These tools help reduce stress resulting from poor planning, mistakes, conflicts with others, and hard work. We shall explore tools that will help you solve your work related problems by maintaining a balanced body and mind through relaxation.

You can influence your body's chemistry

Imagine that you are calmly sitting at your desk reading a business journal. It is three o-clock in the afternoon, and you feel relaxed, lazy and a little bored. You are quite satisfied with what you have done today. As you let your imagination wander, you are suddenly struck by a thought: You are half an hour late for a meeting with the senior staff, to whom you were scheduled to present plans to buy another company! You realize that the president of your organization has been sitting in the conference room, waiting for you since two thirty. Your heart starts to beat faster. Beads of sweat form on your forehead. Your hands go cold, and you have a funny feeling in your stomach. It is hard to think straight. You can not decide what to do. You wonder if you should admit your mistake, blame someone else, get your papers and rush to the board room, or pretend that you have been taken ill. You are also becoming concerned about how your body is now reacting, and about your physical condition.

This example demonstrates how easily your body reacts to a potentially stressful situation. You don't need to be directly in contact with an external threat for your body to react as if you were. The chemical changes which your body undergoes can be triggered by your own thoughts, then it should be possible to reduce stress in the same way.

Stress is not caused by a germ, a virus or a blow to your head. It is a reaction that is triggered by a thought in your brain. In the example above, the changes that take place in you body are caused by the thought that you missed an important meeting. The stress condition is self-inflicted and not caused by any outside force. You have called it into existence.

Now let us imagine that you realized that you made a mistake, and the meeting is not scheduled until tomorrow. With a sigh of relief, the stress symptoms begin to disappear. You return to your reading as if nothing has happened.

Not many years have passed since modern science recognized that the processes of the body are influenced by the processes of the mind. Anxiety, depression and aggressive feelings allowed to grow can lead to physical symptoms. By learning how to change emotions, we can learn how to control the symptoms.

In the next chapter, we will examine several methods for regaining control over our emotions. We can begin by learning to relax and to experience harmony whenever we choose to. The only tool we need is the power of our own thoughts.

15 Relaxation

Given the right circumstances, we can all relax. The degree to which we can relax however, depends upon our environment, our state of mind, and our skills at relaxing. Relaxation skills and techniques have been developed, practiced, improved, and taught for generations throughout the world. They have focused on every conceivable part of the human body and mind, from sole to soul, in search of deeper and deeper levels of relaxation. As the world shrinks to a global community, we have an excellent opportunity to discover the most successful techniques that have been developed to achieve the deepest states of relaxation.

Deep relaxation is a state in which the mind and the body can best be repaired, refreshed, and regenerated. There are several methods of achieving deep relaxation. Methods that have developed from our Western culture often require the help of another person. Such methods include hypnosis and biofeedback. Other methods for achieving deep relaxation include meditation, self-hypnosis, prayer, breathing exercises, and listening to relaxation tapes.

There are many reasons why deep relaxation is enjoyable. First, you gain control of unpleasant stress. Second, by knowing how easily you can attain a peaceful mental state, you feel well prepared to face other difficult situations. Third, by allowing yourself to come into contact with thoughts and physiological functions that might otherwise be ignored, you will gain greater understanding and respect for yourself.

A number of physiological changes occur during a state of deep relaxation. The heart rate slows down. Breathing decreases. Blood pressure drops. Muscular tension is reduced. The alpha waves of the brain increase, signifying a decrease in certain types of brain activity. You enter an entirely different state from that of sleeping or sitting still. As you reach a state of deep relaxation, you are temporarily freed from stress. Upon its completion, you feel relaxed, at peace, refreshed, and energized. You do not escape your stressors, but your ability to deal with difficult situations increases. As a result, you are less damaged by stressors.

Meditation

Meditation is one of the oldest and most effective methods for dealing with stress. It is an art practiced by over half of the world's population. As incredible as it may seem, most Western managers are oblivious to its techniques and benefits. The most noticeable effects of meditation include the slowing down of breathing and the lowering of the activity of the heart. The state that is achieved is the exact opposite of what occurs during stress. Through meditation we are able to counteract the influence of the sympathetic nervous system on the body.

There are many ways to meditate. If you have never meditated before, you may find the following method a good way to begin. Find a place where you can be alone. Sit in a comfortable position and close your eyes. Meditation involves both relaxation and concentration. One particularly effective way to concentrate is to focus your thoughts on nothing but a single specific word. Whatever you choose that word to be, that word is called a mantra. It is most effective when it has no specific meaning; it should invoke no associations. The word "om" is perhaps the most commonly used mantra in the world. It may be appropriate for you to use if it does not make you think of anything in particular. But you can be equally successful by using a word like "zero" or "nothing" as a mantra.

Choose a mantra, and say it quietly to yourself. Repeat it over and over, until you are thinking about nothing else. If thoughts wander in and out of your head while you are meditating, let

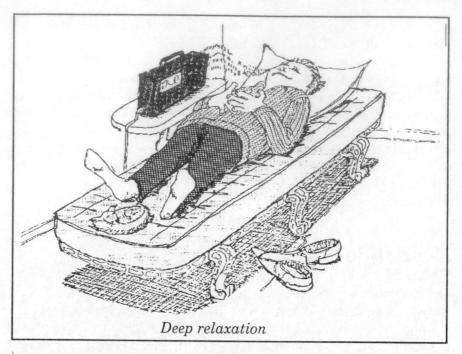

Deep relaxation

them come and go as they will. Do not resist them or encourage them. As you continue to concentrate on your mantra, your mind will begin to clear itself of all thoughts, emotions, images, and stress.

The more you practice your mantra, the greater your ability to concentrate will become. Which each session, you will find it easier to reach a state of relaxation, free from interfering thoughts. Do not attempt to use your mantra to get rid of your thoughts by force. Instead, proceed in a gentle way. If you find that your mind lingers on memories of your childhood, let it do so. Watch thoughts come and go as if they were images on a screen. Do not become involved in them, but think only of your mantra. After a while you can call upon your mantra to gently get rid of destructive and interfering thoughts that may stick in your mind.

Meditation is most effective when it is practiced twice a day, for about 15 minutes each time. When you are ready to begin meditation, get started. Sit where you won't be disturbed, close your eyes, and begin to repeat your mantra quietly to yourself. After some practice, thinking your mantra will work as well as repeating it to yourself. Every time you meditate, you will enter a deeper level of relaxation. After your meditation is over, sit quietly for a moment and allow yourself to enjoy the healthy and stress free state you have reached. You will find these moments of meditation so enjoyable that you will look forward to them every day. If your sympathetic nervous system is overactive, this simple activity will help to calm it down. The long lasting effects of meditation will help to increase the stability of your autonomic nervous system.

Relaxation tapes

We have found that some people do not have the patience to meditate. They prefer to be guided to a state of relaxation by instructions. Recorded instructions for relaxation on commercially available cassette tapes can prove to be very helpful for such people. By following the instructions on the cassette, a state of deep relaxation can be achieved in a fairly short time. The more you listen to such tapes, the easier it is to reach a state of relaxation. Gradually you learn to achieve this state without the tape.

Self-hypnosis

Another technique to help you reach a state of deep relaxation is self-hypnosis. This method is based upon methods of self-suggestion. To practice this technique, sit in a comfortable position, and slowly begin to cross your eyes. Close your eyes, take a deep breath, and then breathe out slowly. Keeping your eyes closed, let your eyes muscles return to normal. Breathe in deeply several times and then breathe out slowly. While breathing slowly, silently repeat to yourself "deeper, deeper". Relax all of your muscles. While continuing to breathe slowly try to imagine yourself sitting in an elevator, going further down every time you say "deeper". After a while you can repeat any suggestions you would like to remember. You may suggest to yourself that you would like to be more relaxed, happier, socially more secure, or any other objective thing that is important to you.

Do not expect immediate results from this method. Results come gradually. Regardless of the kind of hypnosis you use, an optimistic attitude regarding how it will effect you, is necessary for it to work. However skilled a hypnotist may be, it is virtually impossible to be put into a state of trance against your will. Hypnotists achieve the best results with people who want changes to happen.

Part F

You are doing fine

16 Leading others

Management programs and courses alone cannot make a person a good manager. Personalities cannot be easily modified. Good managers are made of "the right stuff". A manager with an unsuitable personality can never outperform a manager who has "the right stuff", no matter how many programs or courses he attends.

The performance of managers can be improved, however, by giving managers the right tools to work with, making them aware of those tools, and teaching them how to use those tools effectively. Successful management programs teach managers how to develop themselves. The more managers can develop themselves, the more they are able to develop their employees. Tools such as the Self Starter, the notebook, and the file binder help managers work in a more determined and effective way. The time managers gain as a result of working more efficiently can be used to develop their employees.

In the following sections we will explore what "the right stuff" is that good managers are made of and how good management programs can develop good managers.

Increase your self-knowledge

The better you know yourself, the better you can manage others. As you continue to learn about your own strengths and the areas in which you can improve, you will be more prepared to develop yourself. As you do so, it becomes easier to appreciate and accept yourself as the person you really are. This is particularly important, as the foundation on which you build your personal and work goals must be firmly attached to reality.

It is not easy to face ourselves. It is even harder if we fail to realize that most people lack the courage to face themselves. Becoming aware that it takes courage to do this takes some of the pressure off us, and provides us with greater energy for the difficult task of seeing ourselves as we really are.

Accept yourself as a manager!

The person who finds it most difficult to accept you as a manager stares at you in the mirror every morning. A recent study indicates that the majority of competent managers secretly fear that they are not competent, and that their organizations will find out that they are incompetent. Your staff accept your authority as a manager, and follow your instructions. You must not disappoint them by avoiding the responsibilities that have been entrusted to you.

Three areas to sink your teeth into

Managers must have three kinds of effective skills. They must have technical skills, administrative skills, and skills to direct and develop staff.

Most managers begin to rise through the ranks because they are skilled in their technical areas. Their subject area knowledge rarely needs to be questioned. They can recognize the difference between good and poor quality production. Questions that are brought to their attention keep them on top of issues related to their own expertise.

Administrative skills are also important for managers. These skills include planning and controlling work. Given the right support and training, most managers can develop their administrative skills.

Managers have the greatest difficulty developing effective skills for directing and managing staff. This group of skills deserves more of our attention.

151

Look under your carpet!

Problems relating to the management and development of staff, and to relationships with staff, are often swept under the carpet. These problems often fall into the category of "important but not urgent". Many managers believe that it is easier to live with their problems than to deal with them. But as with all important matters, the longer they are postponed, the more dangerous they will become. To develop your managerial skills, you must also develop your abilities to direct, develop and relate to your staff. By using the resources within this book, this is not hard to do.

As you begin to pay more attention to staff related problems, you will realize the extent to which you can affect their enthusiasm and motivation. The work climate which you help set in the office can affect how productive your employees will be. The first step towards improving the climate in the office is to pay attention to the present climate. The more attention you pay to staff related issues in the office, the more involved you and your employees will become in resolving problems that may exist. As such problems are resolved, more energy can be devoted to effectively completing the work at hand. The easier work can be completed, the more content everyone in the office will be.

Show the way

A big step can be taken toward reducing staff related problems by showing your employees how to use techniques described in this book. Encouraging them to use devices such as the Self Starter may stimulate conversations about taking responsibility for one's own work. The more responsibilities your employees are willing to take, the more mature a work force you will have for your organization. If you put a few hours aside every month to review your staff's work, you will be amazed by the number of useful suggestions you will get from them.

It is to your mutual advantage that your staff become as familiar with the tools and techniques discussed in this book as you are. The more techniques you are all familiar with, the more you and your staff will be on the same level regarding managing work, and the more you will speak the same language.

How could communication be improved?

Poor communication is the most common cause of staff related problems. Disagreements and poor relationships are often the result of misunderstandings between individuals. Misunderstandings may result from the way we communicate our ideas, as well as from what we communicate. Misunderstanding between individuals can be reduced by using a technique that allows us to see how we communicate, and helps us to understand how the way we communicate affects other people. The techniques described in the next chapter is derived from an area of psychology called Transactional Analysis (TA). You will find this technique helpful for reducing misunderstandings and arguments both in your job and at home.

17 Communicating with others

Management consultants believe that some of the greatest problems at work come from poor planning and poor cooperation among employees. We have discussed many ways to improve planning in this book by gaining greater control over ourselves and our work. We have discussed how to choose the tasks which give us the best results, how to get started on projects, and how to store and retrieve important information. As we continue to discuss the role of the manager, we shall give more attention to the relationships of the manager to his or her fellow employees.

If you have been following the advice in this book, you are working in a more relaxed environment, with more opportunities to pay attention to the needs of other people. To make good use of your opportunities and to understand the needs of other people, we shall explore a technique called Transactional Analysis (TA). TA provides us with a simple and effective method for understanding how people react to one another at home, as well as in the office.

Every year thousands of management programs are presented throughout the world. Few of these programs provide managers with an effective way to resolve conflicts or improve relationships with their employees. With all the theory these programs provide regarding management styles and types, managers are rarely able to bring what they learn in the classroom back to their jobs. On the contrary, poorly taught information can confuse managers. When they try to use it, it can make them less competent in their supervisory responsibilities. A skilled, proud, but authoritarian manager can become very frustrated when attempting to change his or her style to a more democratic one. If the attempt is unsuccessful, the manager may decide to reject all future attempts for self development or staff development. This can cause a number of problems for an organization.

An alternative approach to programs requiring managers to change their style or personalities is to educate managers in Transactional Analysis. TA is a flexible technique designed to help managers benefit from their natural management style in different types of situations. It improves relationships between people by improving communication between them. No attempts are made to change anyone's personality. TA is a time tested technique that has been in use in the United States and in Europe for several decades. It is used to improve many types of relationships, from marriages to corporate partnerships. By widening our minds, and making us aware of our prejudices, it rids us of a good deal of rubbish that can soil our decision making skills. We are able to achieve greater emotional and intellectual insights, and are less inclined to make irrational emotional decisions. As we learn to constructively express our feelings, we become more confident about making decisions for ourselves.

Our different ego states

Transactional Analysis is not hard to understand. It is concerned with the development of the human ego. Each of us has an ego that has taken many years to develop. The ego is the part of us that determines who we are, and decides what we shall do next. The ego of a young child, weighs the child's craving for a cookie "Now!", against a conscience insisting that treats cannot be eaten until after dinner. The ego may solve this conflict by deciding that half the cookie can be eaten now, and the other half can be saved for after the dinner.

Transactional Analysis teaches that the ego can be thought of as having three different parts. The Infant Ego is the part that demands the cookie "Now!". The Parental Ego insists that the cookie can only be eaten at a specified time. The Adult Ego makes a rational decision after taking a number of things into consideration. The way we react to other people or different situations depends on the ego state that happens to be active at a particular time.

The Parental Ego (P-), (P+)

The Parental Ego is concerned with the attitudes and values that parents try to instil in young children. It is associated with terms such as "You must not", You are not allowed", "no", "Stop it", "You ought to be ashamed of yourself", and "Trust no one". There are two types of parental ego states. The first type, called the Oppressive Parental Ego state (P-) is concerned with oppressing our actions. The other type, called the Supportive Parental Ego state (P+), represents the nursing and caring side of the ego.

The Adult Ego (A)

The Adult Ego helps us to make sound and correct decisions. It begins to develop during our first year of life. As it matures, our decisions tend to be less influenced by hostile feelings and prejudices. As we continue to gain experience, we are better able to think and act in a logical manner, giving fair weight to the many factors that go into effective decision making.

The Infant Ego (I)

Any feeling or impulse that comes naturally to an infant is associated with the Infant Ego. Happiness, anger, jealousy, fear, or any other emotion can appear with little warning. This state also includes curiosity.

What do you have on your tapes

The way we behave in a particular situation is largely determined by the ego state we happen to be dominated by at that time.

If you are standing in a telephone booth, cursing the phone because it is out of order, your Infant Ego is fully active. If you are winning a debate at a conference, your Adult Ego is at work. If you hit your leg with a clenched fist on your way home after the debate, because you forget to bring up a point that you felt was important, your Parental Ego is at work.

The three ego states are like recordings on three tape recorders we carry inside ourselves. The Parental Ego records and plays back our parents' concern that "You must", "You ought to", "You must not". The Adult Ego records and plays back the knowledge and experiences we manage to acquire. The Infant Ego includes a record of vivid emotional experiences. All three ego states can be switched on and off to respond to the situations we happen to be involved in. Your Infant Ego is active when you feel and act as you did when you were a child. Your Parental Ego is active when you think, feel, and act as you imagine your parents did when you were young. Your Adult Ego is active when you think rationally, store and use information and facts and make decisions in an objective way.

Different kinds of transactions

When people communicate with each other, their egos interact. Whenever the egos of two people interact, a transaction is said to occur. The kind of interaction depends on the ego state each person is in at the time. When a husband and wife discuss whereto go on their summer vacation, we can expect that the transaction that takes place is between two Adult Egos. If a transaction between two people occurs as expected, it is called a complementary transaction. If a person sending a message gets an answer from a different ego state than the one he or she expected, transactional lines will cross, and it will become difficult to communicate. In order to develop our communication skills, we shall take a closer look at complementary and crossed transactions.

Complementary transactions

A complementary transaction occurs when a person in a certain ego state sends a message to another person, and gets an answer in an expected ego state. When this happens, communication that is transacting between two people can continue without interruption. At that time, the transactional lines are said to be parallel. Below are some examples of parallel complementary transactions. The diagram preceding each example indicates the ego state each person is in during the transaction, and the direction the parallel lines of communication travel in. For each example, the individual on the left is the one who starts to communicate.

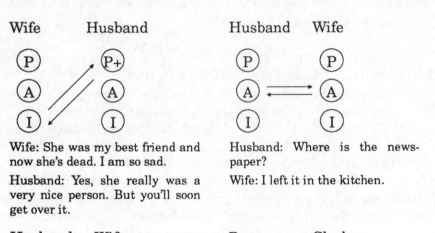

Wife: She was my best friend and now she's dead. I am so sad.

Husband: Yes, she really was a very nice person. But you'll soon get over it.

Husband: Where is the newspaper?

Wife: I left it in the kitchen.

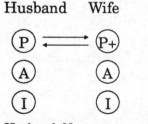

Husband: Now our youngest child is leaving home.

Yes, it's really sad.

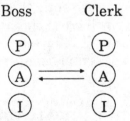

Boss: What time is it?

Clerk: A quarter past three.

Boss   Accountant   Salesman A Salesman B

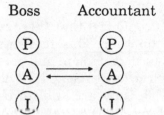
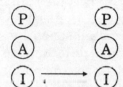

Boss: How can we reduce the year-ly deficit?

Accountant: We'll have to increase our reserve stock.

Salesman A: I don't want to sell any more today. What shall we do?

Salesman B: Let's have a drink.

Husband   Wife   Student   Tutor

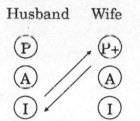
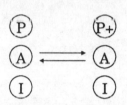

Husband: I've got a temperature. I feel really ill.

Wife: Cheer up dear, you'll soon be better, I'll get you a hot honey drink.

Student: I get so nervous in a new class.

Tutor: Just take it easy and you'll be OK. I'll help you if you have any problems.

Husband   Wife

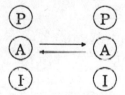

Husband: Where's the bottle opener?

Wife: It's in the top drawer.

As long as the lines of communication are parallell to each other, transactions between people can continue without problems. There is no need for people to defend themselves from one another.

Crossed transactions

Communication becomes difficult when people feel that there is a need to defend themselves from one another. This happens when an individual sends a message to another person, and gets an answer from a different ego state than the one expected. If the transactional lines are no longer parallel, they are said to be crossed. Communication may be broken by quarrels, changing subjects, or by withdrawing from the situation. Below are some examples of crossed transactions. The diagram preceding each example indicates the ego state each person is in during the transaction, and how the lines of communication cross in each situation. As in the previous examples, the individual on the left is the one who starts to communicate.

Wife   Husband

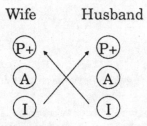

Wife: She was my best friend and now she's dead.

Husband: But what about me? I lost three of my best friends in the army.

Husband   Wife

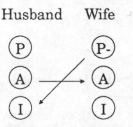

Husband: Where's the bottle opener?

Wife: Probably where you put it. Look for it yourself.

Salesman A Salesman B

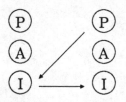

Salesman A: Now we've sold enough. What shall we do now?

Salesman B: We should complete the monthly report.

Wife   Husband

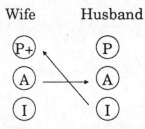

Wife: I need the car tonight since I'm going to visit my mother.

Husband: Why don't you ever spend an evening with me?

There is a time and a place for each ego state to be active. Our (P+) Parental Ego can show sympathy to people around us. Our Infant Ego allows us to be playful or dependent. Our Adult Ego helps us test reality. Problems come when transactions between people cross in unexpected ways.

Dominant states

Some people get stuck in a single ego state. They always seem to respond to others as a parent, child, or adult. It is difficult to interact with people who can respond only with the single state they are caught in. We tend to identify those people with the state they are dominated by.

Always a parent

People dominated by the Parental Ego tend to treat co-workers as children. They often have authoritarian personalities, and may appear to be too dominating (P-) or supportive (P+). They are attracted to careers as policemen, soldiers, teachers, and health practitioners.

Always an adult

People dominated by the Adult Ego tend to put a tremendous amount of weight on facts. They are often accused of being cold and calculating. They may be attracted to careers in engineering, accounting, mathematics, and computer sciences.

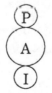

Always an infant
People who are dominated by the Infant Ego often avoid taking responsibility for their own actions. They do not like to make decisions. They are often attracted to careers in acting.

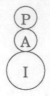

How to use TA
How can TA help you manage your life better?

The more you know about yourself, the better equipped you are to manage your life. The more you can recognize your own tendencies towards a particular ego state, the better you can correct and prevent your own inappropriate behavior. A knowledge of Transactional Analysis puts you in a position to learn about the prejudices and assumptions of your Parent Ego, about the fears of your Adult Ego, and about the interests of your Adult Ego. You can develop your Adult Ego to improve decision making skills. The more you learn about yourself, the greater respect you will have for yourself.

TA also gives you a better understanding of the relationships you are involved in. TA has been used for marriage counselling in the United States for decades. By identifying their dominant ego states and the way they react to one another, partners can determine how to improve their relationship. A manager who is familiar with TA can recognize the ego needs of his or her employees. Once those needs are recognized, the manager can respond to them to get work done. By keeping lines of transactions parallel, confrontations can be avoided. A supportive Parental Ego can communicate to immature employees. Managers who build Adult-Adult transactions among their employees benefit by gaining a more mature work force.

A word of cation must be given about TA. A little knowledge can be a dangerous thing. Don't misuse your understanding of TA to hurt or embarrass others. It may be tempting to accuse an opponent in an argument that he is stuck in his parental or infant ego. But this tactic will do little good. Instead, it is to your mutual advantage to use your knowledge of TA to promote co-operation and understanding between you and those with whom you wish to communicate.

A manager's conclusion about TA

TA helps us understand problems that can occur when people try to communicate. It also helps us understand how we can avoid confrontations and manage people in more effective ways. We can keep transaction lines parallel by being aware of our own ego states of our employees. The better we can communicate with our employees, the better our relationships will be with them, the fewer confrontations we will have, the more effective we can be at work, and the more time we will have to enjoy life.

18 Motivating others

Transactional Analysis gives us a model to help us understand how people communicate and react in different situations. The model becomes even more useful when we connect it to another one. This second model was developed by Maslow, a well-known psychologist, to help us understand how and why people are motivated. It identifies the needs all people have, and the order or hierarchy in which these needs occur. Together, these models will help you gain a greater understanding of how to motivate your employees, so that you may manage them more effectively.

The hierarchy of needs

Maslow first presented the idea that people are motivated by a hierarchy of needs, in the fifties. The diagram on page 165 illustrates the needs people have, and the hierarchy in which they occur. Needs located towards the bottom of the diagram must be satisfied first. Once physiological needs are met, the next need to emerge is the need for security. Needs emerge in the order they are presented in Maslow's hierarchy. But a need will not emerge until the ones below it have been satisfied.

A person who is broke and unemployed will not be as concerned about interpersonal relationships as he is about security. Once he gets a job and his need for security is satisfied, he will begin to seek appreciation from others. If he is able to satisfy that need through his work, he will try to get involved in more

SELF FULFILLMENT

APPRECIATION

BELONGING

SECURITY

HUNGER THIRST

Maslow's hierarchy of needs

things that interest him, and that he is suited to do. At this point, his strongest need is for self-fulfillment.

People are motivated by their needs. Your employees will not be motivated if they believe that their needs cannot be met. A good manager gives his employees job assignments that make it possible for them to meet their own needs, as well as the needs of the organization.

Your choice

If you are not satisfied with your work life, your work may not be meeting your needs. If you work does not offer you the opportunity to meet your needs, and nothing can be done to change the situation, you might consider another job.

We know a high school teacher who has been teaching for fifteen years. As the years pass, he finds it more and more difficult to come to work. He gets through his lessons by detaching himself from what he is doing. He does not spend more time with his colleagues than he has to. When he tries hard, his efforts are unappreciated and unrewarded. The only need his job satisfies is for security. How does he feel about work? Obviously, not too good. Maslow's model teaches us that an individual who is not able to meet his needs can not feel satisfaction.

What happens when needs are not satisfied?

Many problems can occur if needs are not satisfied. We have seen how stress and stress symptoms can result in a number of illnesses. Individuals suffering from these symptoms cannot do anything about them if they do not understand the problems. Unable to change their life, they accept their troubles like sheep waiting to be slaughtered.

Suppose that by chance the teacher we have referred to gets a job as a research assistant in a new company. He becomes part of a team which succeeds in accomplishing noticeable achievements in an interesting field. Within months, his hierarchy of needs are met, including his need for self-fulfillment. He is highly motivated, interested in his work, and feels happy. His stress symptoms disappear. He has become a different person, and you would probably not recognize him if you happened to run across him in the street. Before, he was half-dead. Now he is sparkling with vitality. As we stare at the changed person in front of us, we begin to understand Maslow's theory of the hierarchy of needs.

Moving along

You now have two models to guide you in your efforts to become a better manager.

Transactional Analysis will help you make better and more rational decisions, improve communication with your employees, and understand relationships at work. Maslow's hierarchy of needs will help you to motivate your employees and understand your own needs. As you combine the knowledge you gain from these models with your new skills to direct your own work, you will have many opportunities to become a better manager.

In the next chapter, we shall examine one more problem managers commonly face. In the programs we teach, we often get questions about how managers can effectively criticize their employees when it is necessary to do so. The art of criticism is an important skill for a manager to have. We shall now explore some methods for developing this skill.

19 Criticizing others

Managers find it very difficult to criticize employees. There are many reasons for this. Some managers are concerned about hurting the feelings of their employees. Others are afraid of destroying a pleasant atmosphere at work. Some are afraid that they themselves will be criticized if they criticize others. Still others just don't know how to criticize employees.

Whether or not they realize it, all managers criticize their employees in many ways. A manager who is dissatisfied with an employee cannot hide such concerns for any period of time. The manager's body language and tone of voice will communicate his or her feelings. Managers who bite their lips and avoid dealing with problem employees are not doing their job.

Imagine that you have an employee who is always late for work. You have avoided the unpleasant task of confronting him about this problem. Instead, you become more and more irritated about it. Your employee is unaware of your concern, and does not realize why you are so upset. Eventually, your anger explodes, making people wonder why you cannot control your temper.

How could you avoid this unpleasant situation? Some managers who have trouble criticizing their employees handle such problems by looking for opportunities to praise them when they perform as they should. They may attempt to correct a lateness problem by praising an employee when he is on time. Their intention is to make the employee understand that it is important to be on time.

Although this method can be effective, it is only a coping tech-nique. It offers no help when an employee must actually be criticized.

As a manager, you have a right and an obligation to criticize employees who are not performing their jobs as they should. You have a right to tell an employee how his or her unsatisfactory performance concerns you. You have a right to tell employees what you expect from them, and what will happen if those expec-tations are not met. If you are to be effective as a manager, you must be able to assert your rights as a manager.

Help me

An assertive manager would tell the problem employee in our example: "I become concerned and annoyed when you continue to be late for work. I would appreciate it if you would spare me such feelings". This makes it clear to the employee what actions upset the manager, what the consequences of such actions are and what must be done to correct the problem. If the employee is mature and worth keeping, he will try to please the manager by being on time in the future.

Write it down!

Another way to deal with the problem employees is to write down what you expect them to do, and refer them to the written expectations if problems occur. By doing this, you clarify your own thoughts, identify what it is you want them to do, and set up a device to determine how well they have met agreed upon ex-pectations. Written job descriptions and performance appraisal standards can be used for this purpose. Offer letters for new em-ployees can also be used to emphasize what you expect of your employees.

If an employee is seldom on time, you may say to him: "Have you forgotten about item three on our agreement? I don't think you are respecting our agreement about being on time". In this way, you make clear to the employee that the issue of being late centres around an agreement that has been made, rather than a personality issue. It is not necessary for either of you to become upset over the matter.

These are some methods to make it easier for you to criticize employees when it is necessary to do so. These methods are not meant to remove all discomforts managers experience when they criticize their employees. A person who finds no difficulty in criticizing others lacks respect for the feelings of others, and lacks the human qualities that are required to be a successful manager.

Enough about management

We have given enough time to the problems of management. You will have no trouble succeeding as a manager as you use the techniques and tools presented in this book, consciously work to reduce stress, and develop your skills to motivate and give feedback to others. Keep your transactional communication lines parallel, and try to assign and delegate work to your employees in a way that meets their needs, as well as the needs of the organization. As you reduce your own stress, you will reduce stress within your organization. As your employees become less distressed, they will be able to contribute more to getting work done.

Part G

The power of your thoughts

The Power of your thoughts

So far, our presentation has been very sensible and rational. It is time to pause and do some reality testing. We must determine if the ideas we have presented feel right. If we find a contradiction that cannot be resolved between what our brains says and what our heart feels, our heart must win. Our feelings must be in harmony with our reasoning. If they are not, they will work against each other. It is not possible to manage one's life in such discord.

20 Choose your feelings

To some extent, it is possible to control what you feel. Your thoughts can help you accomplish this, As you learn how to use them, you will gain control over emotions such as anger, remorse, jealousy, anxiety and guilt. Psychologists have known for many years that what you feel emotionally greatly depends on the thoughts you are having. Anger turned against yourself becomes guilt. Guilt to a target outside of yourself becomes anger. You can laugh away your fears.

In chapter 14, we presented an example of an unpleasant situation: We asked how you would feel if you had missed a meeting with your senior management. Just imagine such a situation is stressful. But you can influence your imagination by your thoughts. Let's consider another example. You arrive home from work expecting that your partner has cleaned the house and washed the dishes, as you had agreed. But you discover that nobody is home and nothing has been done. At first you get very angry with your partner for breaking your agreement. A moment later you are struck by the thought that your partner may have had to drive to the hospital with one of your children and your anger is replaced by anxiety. Then you remember that your partner had to drive the car to the garage for repairs, and will be home soon. Now you anxiety disappears and you feel guilty for being quick tempered.

Every feeling you experienced in this example was a direct result of your thoughts.

A bundle of energy

As we have seen, having the right tools is not all that is needed to get your work in order. You must also develop self-discipline. Self-discipline is also necessary for controlling feelings that can be counterproductive to your success. Of course it is neither possible nor desirable to control all of our feelings. But it is to our advantage to be able to deal with the emotions that stand in our way of managing life as we would like.

Imagine that all of your energy is put in a big sack. Every time you experience a counterproductive feeling, some energy escapes through a tiny hole in the sack. If you learn to minimize your counterproductive feelings, you can conserve and use energy that would otherwise be lost.

If we can control our feelings, we can be responsible for them. It is a responsibility that we should not run away from. If we do run from it, we provide other people with the power to influence our feelings. We know a teacher who has the dubious ambition to be popular with all of his pupils. This is an impossible expectation. Every pupil has unique needs, wishes, and motives that will influence the way a teacher is perceived. One pupil may find a particular teacher marvelous, while another pupil thinks that the same teacher should choose another profession. In every class there will be at least one pupil who will speak critically about teachers in general. To summarize, this teacher's goal to be liked by all students is unrealistic, and will result in disappointment and other counterproductive feelings if it is not controlled.

The lesson to learn from this example can be applied to any organization. A manager who is too concerned about being popular with all his employees can never be content with his or her interpersonal skills. We doubt that the managers that you admire are overly concerned about being popular with all employees.

Believe in yourself

What can the teacher in our example do to regain control over his feelings? The answer is simple. He must realize that he has a job to do that must be done as he believes it should be done. He must face the fact that some pupils will appreciate his efforts, while others may not. He can avoid unnecessary loss of energy only after realizing that he "can't please everyone, so he's got to please himself".

Do not give other people responsibility for your feelings. If you should feel guilty, angry, or anxious, say to yourself "I've chosen to feel anger because..." Don't say that you are angry with someone because he or she did so and so. By taking responsibility for your anger, you are putting yourself in a position to control it. By choosing not to perceive another person as responsible for your feelings, you will be able to work out problems in your relationships in more successful ways. If couples learned to think this way, the majority of all marriage problems could disappear.

Do like Bjorn Borg!

Bjorn Borg followed our advice. He did not allow himself to become confused in a tennis match. Regardless of the tricks used by his opponents, he did not give them control over the way he felt during a game.

Let us consider another example. Imagine that you are looking out of a window in your home just as your spouse carelessly backs your car into a tree in your garden. You get angry about this careless action, and angrier still as you remember your partner's previous careless driving record. But your training in Transactional Analysis makes you realize that you are thinking like a condemning parent. Understanding the consequences of confronting your spouse from this viewpoint, you begin to get a grip on your anger. You decide to handle the situation by discussing it with your spouse as an adult to an adult. You remember what you have read about taking responsibility for your own feelings. You decide to use your thoughts to control your feelings. Because you choose to think warmly about your partner, and are unable to hold more than one thought at a time, positive thoughts begin to dominate your mind. You reason that you too were responsible for this accident, as you chose to buy a large car with a limited rear view instead of small and versatile one which your partner preferred.

The way you use your thoughts will help you eliminate counterproductive feelings. You can use your mind to help brighten up your days. As you learn to use your thoughts as a tool, you will wonder why you ever allowed yourself to be controlled by counterproductive feelings that sapped you of energy. Your relationships will improve in both your work and personal life.

Think positively

It is easy to identify things that can irritate you. At times, friends, co-workers, neighbors and relatives can be the source of irritation. If you do not use your thoughts to manage your feelings, you will become a victim of your emotions on a regular basis. But if you ask yourself "Is an argument worth the trouble?" before you have one, you may save yourself a lot of time, energy, and aggravation. It makes more sense to save your resources for important things, and to think positively.

You can become what you want to

In many ways, you are what you think you are. If you have a high opinion of yourself, others will treat you accordingly. If you don't think well of yourself, you can't expect that other people will. An important ingredient for success is to have a positive view of yourself.

You will recall that we often think in images rather than in words. We use words to create images for people we talk with. If you tell people that you have visited California they may have images of beaches, palm trees, and cars. In a way, as we talk to others, we project images into their brain. The more we are aware of this, the sharper we can focus those images when we want to.

Show them exciting films

If you are a manager who has a problem that can only be solved with the help of your employees, it is important that you motivate them to solve it. You can begin to gain their interest in solving the problem by projecting exciting images into their minds.

If you say to them "There is a problem that we should work on", you may not get much attention from them. But if you say, "We are about to begin an exciting job, which we may find quite a challenge to accomplish", you project images involving sport and excitement to them. You will catch their interest and harness their skills. As the pen is mightier than the sword, words can capture the imagination and enthusiasm of your employees. Do not use them thoughtlessly.

Positive words and thoughts will project positive images into the minds of others. Keep a positive attitude towards clients, vendors, and professionals you meet with, and the chances are that they will keep a positive attitude towards you. Before meeting with clients, use the power of your thoughts to focus on the points you like about them. You might recall something they did which you appreciated.

When you meet them, you will then find it easy to be friendly to them. In turn they will find it easier to be friendly towards you. The positive atmosphere you have helped to create will contribute to good communication between you.

Smile and feel well

Emile Coué was a chemist who lived during the second half of the 19th century. He was interested in the powers of the mind. Coué recognized the importance of the imagination for influencing thoughts and feelings. He observed that when the imagination and the will were in conflict, imagination would win. It is easy, for example, to walk on a balance beam which is lying on the ground. Your imagination will not interfere with this action. But if the board is placed high above the ground between the roofs of two houses, you would probably be afraid to cross it. You might imagine that after you take a few steps, you would fall.

Scientists at the University of California have demonstrated that people who are ill feel better when they can get themselves to smile or laugh. They have suggested that facial expressions involved in smiling can influence the nervous system, as well as one's feelings. If you feel irritable when you wake up in the morning, inject yourself with pleasant thoughts. If you can imagine that it will be a beautiful day, you'll soon feel better. The phrase "Every day in every way I'm getting better and better" was inspired by the ideas of Emile Coué. When your imagination and your will are in accord, it is possible to do great things.

Part H

Group exercises

Group exercises

It is easy to discuss issues about career and staff development when you are with other managers. It is an area in which there is wide interest and significant needs. In the next chapter we will present some group exercises and discussions to help improve life at work. Some of the exercises are designed to improve your own work, while others are designed to achieve better cooperation between the members of your organization. If you involve your co-workers in them, you will contribute to improving the working atmosphere in your office.

21 A wealth of experiences

A vast source

The exercises in this chapter should prove to be both exciting and challenging to you and your department. The material for the exercises is derived from a vast source of experiences, values, attitudes, hopes, and disappointments of you and your co-workers. They are designed to have concrete value for any organization. They do not include boring or meaningless activities that can destroy interest and enthusiasm. They do not depend on films or videos to keep the fire burning during discussions.

After employees within a department have had the opportunity to read this book, someone should accept the responsibility to organize exercises, schedule and plan meetings, and keep a record of who attends. Ideally, meetings should last two hours each followed by members attending lunch together.

If an exercise is completed in less than an hour, begin the next exercise. At the end of each meeting schedule a time for the next one, to be held in a week or two.

If your department consists of more than ten people, the exercises should be performed in two or more groups. Before you begin the exercises, write an outline of the specific points that are to be covered in the exercise, and hand copies out to the participants. If a group exercise results in proposals for changes or improvements in the work of the department, record it in writ-

Group discussion

ing. At the end of each exercise, be sure to determine who will be responsible for implementing any changes that are to be made within your department.

Exercises

Exercise 1
Participants identify some common problems they share within the department. They then discuss how they can work better to reduce or solve the problems they have identified.

Exercise 2
Participants identify the types of crises that tend to recur within the department. They then discuss what influences their choice

of projects to work on, and why it is often so difficult to get started on certain projects.

Exercise 3
Group members help each other develop Self Starters. The manager of the department should be present during this exercise. Because the exercise may take some time to complete, it could be divided into several sessions.

Exercise 4
This exercise should be performed between two meetings. During the week or weeks preceding the exercise, participants should agree that they will attempt to act in a kind, appreciative and supportive way towards each other. As the appreciation for each other should be well founded, flattery is not allowed. When the group meets for exercise 5, members discuss why giving legitimate support to others is a skill which takes time to develop.

Exercise 5
After performing the activities discussed above, the group determines what changes, if any, occurred in the atmosphere at work.

In the second part of this exercise, the department's methods for filing and storing papers should be discussed. Problems and methods for improvement are identified. A specific date should be set for modifying the paper storage system, as described in chapter 10.

Exercise 6
Discuss the problems that result when interruptions occur during the work day.

Exercise 7
Discuss how stress effects life at work and at home. Identify common causes of stress. How do people react under stress? Participants identify their own stress symptoms and what they can do about them. Identify how the relaxation methods described in this book have been of help to the participants.

Exercise 8

This section concerns the participant's reaction to Transactional Analysis. After having read this book each person will have a certain attitude towards it and to the advice it gives. Try to analyze your attitude toward this book by using each of the three different ego states. Before you describe your attitude, determine which ego state is active at that time. Discuss how the different egos influence your opinion of this book and its advice.

Look at the illustrations of Transactional Analysis below. Give some examples of incidents that have occurred within the department, that could be understood with the help of the following illustrations from TA. In all of the illustrations, the transaction starts from individual number 1.

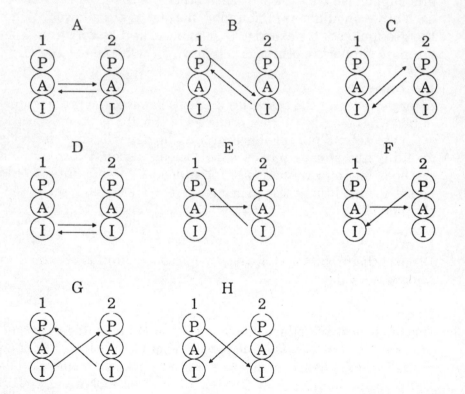

Exercise 9

Discuss what effect the advice from this book has had, or will have on your life.

A concluding remark

Now it only remains for us to wish you good luck. You can use your newly acquired tools and powers of thought to work less - but more wisely.

As time goes on, you may not have to attend as many meetings as you did before. You will be able to delegate more and direct your own work better. The freedom which you have acquired can be used for planning and working towards your own development, as well as the development of the organization or department for which you work.

Maslow has described "peak experiences", as moments when you feel extremely happy. Everything seems just fine. You are not worried about the future, and you feel no bitterness about the past. You experience harmony and happiness. To be able to achieve a peak experience, you must be able to pull yourself from the grip of unsatisfactory circumstances. You have one life; don't live it on a treadmill.

As you work less, you will have more time for other kinds of experiences. These experiences can inspire you to discover additional sides of your personality. As you continue to grow, your life will become fuller and richer with the passage of time.

We suggest that you circulate this book where you work, and that you openly discuss the questions that are brought up.

At times, it may be appropriate to arrange for workshops to stimulate discussions. If that is the case, we would be happy to assist you. The author of this book is a real person who can be reached by phone.

Every day should be enjoyed as if you were on a summer vacation